Teaching adult
second language learners

CAMBRIDGE HANDBOOKS FOR LANGUAGE TEACHERS

This is a series of practical guides for teachers of English and other languages. Illustrative examples are usually drawn from the field of English as a foreign or second language, but the ideas and techniques described can equally well be used in the teaching of any language.

In this series:

Teaching Adult Second Language Learners

Heather McKay

Abigail Tom

CAMBRIDGE
UNIVERSITY PRESS

CAMBRIDGE UNIVERSITY PRESS
Cambridge, New York, Melbourne, Madrid, Cape Town,
Singapore, São Paulo, Delhi, Mexico City

Cambridge University Press
32 Avenue of the Americas, New York, NY 10013–2473, USA

www.cambridge.org
Information on this title: www.cambridge.org/9780521649902

First published 1999
16th printing 2013

Printed in the United States of America

A catalog record for this publication is available from the British Library.

Library of Congress Cataloging in Publication Data
McKay, Heather, 1950–
Teaching adult second language learners / Heather McKay, Abigail H. Tom.
p. cm – (Cambridge handbooks for language teachers)
ISBN 978-0-521-64990-2 (pbk.)
1. Language and languages – Study and teaching. 2. Second language acquisition.
3. Adult education. I. Tom, Abigail, 1941– II. Title. III. Series
P53.M33 1999
418'.0071'5–dc21   99-36775

ISBN 978-0-521-64990-2 paperback

Contents

Contents

Family   55

Community   73

Food   90

Clothing   112

Contents

With thanks to our colleagues and students who have taught us so much.

With thanks also to Penny Ur for her determination to make this book the best that it could be. Any remaining shortcomings are of course our own.

Introduction

Who will use this book?

Throughout the world, people are moving from one country to another. Whether they are immigrants or visitors, most of these people have one thing in common: They must learn a new language in order to survive and thrive in their new environment. As a result, there are thousands of language classes for adult newcomers. There are great differences from one country to another with regard to these classes. In some countries government-sponsored programs are the norm, whereas in others there is a mix of public and private funding. In the case of immigrants, often a limited length of time is allowed for language study before newcomers are expected to be self-sufficient. Although we recognize these differences, we also feel that teachers of second languages to adults have much in common.

This book is intended for you, the teachers of adult second language learners. In it we address general questions concerning lesson organization and content as well as providing specific activities to make your classes more successful. Bearing in mind that in some situations teachers are expected to assess and place students and to organize their own curriculum in addition to teaching, we have included basic information on these topics. Books that provide additional information are listed in the Bibliography.

We have based this book on our own experience and on that of teachers whom we have come to know in our work and at conferences and workshops. We have tried to create activities which are easy enough linguistically for language learners, but which will appeal to adult learners' interests and needs. We hope that you will find it both useful and interesting.

Who is the adult second language learner?

Adults come to a new country for a variety of reasons. Some come simply to learn the language and culture, but most come to work or study. Some come in order to accompany or join family or friends and others to escape from difficult circumstances at home.

Just as reasons for coming vary, so does the length of stay in the new country. Some are short-term visitors, staying for a few months, others stay for a few years, and still others for the rest of their lives. Some, who do not need the language for employment outside their homes and whose family members take care of most of the practical aspects of their lives, attend classes primarily for social reasons. For them, the language class provides a respite from the loneliness of staying at home in a strange country. Others are immigrants who are under pressure to join the workforce as quickly as possible. Still others already have jobs but need to increase their language skills in order to keep or advance in their jobs.

Although these newcomers represent many countries, first languages, and cultures, they still have a number of things in common. They want and need to learn to *use* the language. They need to be able to shop, to bank, to use buses, and to work. To function successfully in their new environment they need to be able to speak to and understand the people around them, as well as read and write.

What do adult learners bring to a class?

Because of the heterogeneous nature of adult classes, it is important to consider the following dimensions.

Language

First, adults already know one language well, and that language is a vital part of their identity and the means through which they relate to others. The newcomer knows the sound and structure systems (and in many cases the written conventions) of his* first language, which both help and hinder learning a new language. In a social sense, using a new language represents a tremendous risk: of being misunderstood, of being corrected, of being laughed at, of feeling embarrassed or childish, and even in some cases of being rejected by one's own compatriots. On the other hand, the need and desire to communicate with others in the new language provides strong motivation for most newcomers.

Background knowledge

In addition to language, adult students bring background knowledge and experience of their own and other cultures as well as knowledge

---

* In order to avoid awkwardness in construction, we have chosen to refer to the learner as masculine and to the teacher as feminine throughout this book. No bias is intended, of course: Many teachers are men and many learners are women.

and experience gained from work or home. This knowledge of the world is a rich resource for the teacher who chooses to exploit it. By drawing on the students' previous knowledge, the teacher not only validates a lifetime of learning but also has a base on which to build new knowledge.

Expectations

These learners also bring with them the attitudes and knowledge developed in previous schooling. Those who have had little schooling and who lack literacy skills in their first language may find language classes intimidating unless a special effort is made to welcome and include them. Those who have studied a second language previously will be influenced by that experience. If they have been successful, they are likely to assume that they will be successful again. Not only will they be more confident, but they will also have developed strategies to help them learn a new language. Students who have had unpleasant or unsuccessful experiences as learners are likely to expect more of the same.

Learners with prior language learning experiences are also likely to bring with them expectations of how language classes should be organized and taught. They may associate language learning exclusively with grammar and translation, and feel threatened when they find that speaking and listening are major features of their new class. If they come from a culture in which the teacher's job is to transmit knowledge, they may feel uncomfortable with group or pair work and may question the validity of a class in which the teacher does not stand in front of the students and lecture. If they are from a culture in which the teacher is considered all-knowing, they may doubt the competence of a teacher who admits to not knowing something. It is important for the teacher to find out what the students' expectations are and to address areas in which the students' expectations differ from the teacher's or from each others'. Differences in expectations may sometimes necessitate that the teacher and students negotiate what and how to learn. In addition, the teacher needs to share with the students the goals and theoretical justifications for specific classroom activities.

Learning styles

Like all learners, adults have different learning styles. Some feel comfortable learning by watching and listening, whereas others feel they cannot learn unless they take down notes and analyze rules. They may also have preferences for learning through different sense modalities: touching, hearing, smelling, tasting, and seeing. The teacher will need to understand and cater to these differences by utilizing cycles of teaching that exploit different learning styles at different points in the lesson. This will also have the advantage of enabling the students to extend their range of learning styles by exposing them to new ones.

Confidence

Adult learners also bring many other personal characteristics, perhaps the most important of which is confidence or the lack thereof. Many students with little initial proficiency leap ahead of their classmates, in large part because they are confident that they can and will learn the language. These students go out and take the risks involved in using the new language to communicate with anyone and everyone they encounter. Others of comparable ability and background may languish at a low level of proficiency because they lack the confidence to use the language. It is therefore very important to provide a supportive classroom atmosphere where risk taking and other positive learning behaviors are fostered.

Motivation

Students also vary considerably in their motivation. One student may want desperately to communicate with his neighbors and coworkers; another may perceive little use for the new language once his basic needs are met. Grades may provide additional motivation for younger students, but this is not the case for most adult second language students. They are not generally required to attend classes nor to take tests. Motivation, then, must come from within them and be based on their perception that what they are learning is of interest and of value to them. For such students the teacher can enhance motivation by providing interesting activities and by making clear the value of what is being taught and its relevance to their goals.

Personal circumstances

Age, health, and other personal circumstances also influence adult learners. Adult classes often include students ranging in age from 18 to 80 or more. Students may feel they have little common ground among them. Younger students may perceive those who are older as slow and rigid, while older adults may feel that younger ones are frivolous and irresponsible. Health, particularly for the older adults, may be a complicating factor. Difficulties with hearing, eyesight, and memory need to be taken into account. A history of arthritis or stroke may make writing difficult. In addition, personal circumstances, such as employment or lack of it, difficulties with child care or transportation, or concerns about problems at home necessarily take priority, making attendance, punctuality, and concentration difficult for some students. Although we may not be able to change the students' personal circumstances, we can, by being flexible and by encouraging a sense of community in the classroom, provide a source of support.

Effective instructors need to inform their teaching by collecting information about their students' first language knowledge, knowledge of the world, previous learning experience, learning styles and preferences, personalities and personal circumstances, as well as their existing second language skills and goals.

How can instructors obtain information about their students?

Initial data collection

In most adult education programs, a great deal of information is collected before the student arrives in the instructor's classroom. Forms are filled out, interviews are conducted, and frequently formal tests are administered to ascertain the student's second language level. In some programs, instructors are involved in these placement procedures, but in others they are not. In either case it is important for the teacher to be aware of the information collected, as it relates to both the student's proficiency level and to his circumstances, goals, and background. In this section we talk about some of the tools that can be used at this initial stage.

FORMAL TESTS

Formal tests provide only a starting point for data collection because they generally focus exclusively on the student's proficiency in the language. It is possible to utilize either a standardized test or one created in-house. Standardized tests have the advantage of being normed across a large population, but an in-house test may provide information which is more pertinent to the particular program in which the student is enrolled. Furthermore, there is often a problem of fit between the adult program's typical focus on language use and the focus on form of many standardized tests. If a standardized test is used, it is important to make sure that it in fact provides information that is appropriate and relevant to the curriculum of the program.

INTERVIEWS

An interview provides another way to assess a student's proficiency while at the same time allowing the teacher to learn more about his background and interests. In an ideal world, the interview should be carried on in a comfortable, quiet, and private setting, free from distractions. In practice a corner of the classroom or the corridor often has to suffice. In any case, it should be made clear to the student that this is an interview. Distractions should be kept to a minimum. The interviewer can create a sense that the student is the center of her attention by arranging chairs so that she and the student can look at each other without barriers such as desks between them. Needless to say, it is important for the interviewer to smile, to focus on, and to respond to the student's answers and not to perform other tasks at the same time. An interview is a time to listen and not a time to correct the student. It is useful to have pictures available to provide lower-level or shy students with visual support. This interview should be done alone, without intervention from friends of the student. Although this placement interview is usually carried out in the second language, it may be appropriate later, in order to learn more about the student's background and expectations, to conduct an additional interview in his first language.

The interviewer can begin by introducing herself. The body of the interview should be arranged from easier to more difficult questions. A possible sequence of questions and cues is provided in Box 1. Begin with formulaic questions concerning personal information. These familiar questions will help the student feel comfortable and will also give the interviewer basic information and an opportunity to ascertain the student's control of functions related to personal identification and verb tenses.

If the student has difficulty answering these questions, the interviewer should try to elicit language by using pictures. Every attempt should be made to allow the student to make some successful response. This includes the use of single-object pictures and yes/no questions.

If the student is successful in the first part of the interview, more difficult open-ended questions should be used. The interviewer should be sensitive to the student's verbal and nonverbal responses to these questions and change the topic if there is evidence of any discomfort. For more advanced students, a challenging task is to make comparisons of countries, cities, jobs, or schools. The interviewer should encourage the student to expand on his answers by use of follow-up questions and judicious silence. When it is clear that the student has reached the limit of his competence, the interviewer should end the interview by thanking the student.

It will, of course, depend on the individual program how students are placed based on the interview, but factors that may be considered are control of functions, structures, and vocabulary; complexity of thought and language, and risk taking. It needs to be taken into account that one student might avoid errors by using only simple vocabulary and structures, whereas another might take greater risks and consequently make more mistakes.

BOX 1

Interview sequence

What is your name?

How do you spell it?

Do you live in _____ (city)?

Do you have a job?

Where are you from?

When did you come to this country?

How long have you been in _____ (city)?

Tell me about your daily routine.

Tell me about your family.

Tell me about your education.

Tell me about your job.

Tell me about your language learning experience.

What do you do in your spare time or on weekends?

What questions would you like to ask about the program?

What are your plans for the future?

What are the main differences between _____
(country of origin) and _____ (country
currently living in)?

What are the main differences between schools (or cities) in
_____ (country of origin) and in
_____ (country currently living in)?

If you could have any job, what would you like to be? (Why?)

I read an article saying that _____

What do you think about that?

7

WRITING SAMPLES

In addition to formal tests and interviews, a writing sample can give further information about literacy and about the student. The student can be given a choice of writing prompts (see Box 2). Alternatively, the student can be assigned a series of tasks of increasing difficulty to be completed in a given time period. Depending on his writing skill, he may or may not complete the entire sequence. The first task might be to fill out a simple form, followed by writing about a picture or sequence of pictures, and finally completing an open-ended writing task based on a topic such as learning English. A third way of eliciting a writing sample is to provide a single task that can be performed at various levels, such as filling in speech balloons in a cartoon.

Ongoing data collection

Once the students are placed and classes begin, the teacher will need to combine information about what the students know, what they want to know, and what the program would like them to know in order to determine what to teach. Because the students are now in the language classroom with the teacher, this information can be collected through language learning activities that are integrated into the curriculum. This does not preclude the use of interviews and writing tasks, but it does open up other possibilities.

BOX 2

Writing prompts

Write about your family.

Write about what you do every day.

Write a letter to your language instructor telling him or her about your past language learning experiences.

Write a letter introducing yourself to other class members.

You are applying for a new job. Describe your past work experience.

Copyright © Cambridge University Press.

FINDING OUT WHAT STUDENTS KNOW ABOUT AND WHAT THEY
CAN DO WITH THE LANGUAGE

1. *Observation.* One of the teacher's most powerful tools in data
   collection is systematic and ongoing observation of student
   performance. This enables the teacher to find out what students
   know about and what they can do with the language. Teachers
   constantly monitor what their students say and how they say it.
   While students are working together in groups, the teacher can walk
   around the class, listen, and take notes. This has the advantage of
   not disrupting the normal flow of classroom activities. Student-made
   tapes and writing assignments provide a way for the teacher to
   monitor oral and written performance outside of class.
2. *Asking questions.* To find out what students can do with the
   language, the teacher can simply ask them. This can be done orally
   or in writing. One technique is to ask students individually or in
   groups to respond to questions on large sheets of paper posted on
   the wall. Each paper should ask one question (see Box 3).

   In a different activity, students can fill in a chart saying what they
   can and cannot do with regard to a particular skill area or topic.

Having ascertained what the students know, the next task is to find
out what they want to learn.

BOX 3

Poster questions

How often do you speak _____ (the
second language)?

How often do you listen to _____ (the
second language)?

How often do you read _____ (the second
language)?

How often do you write _____ (the
second language)?

With whom do you speak?

Where do you speak?

When do you speak?

Introduction

FINDING OUT WHAT STUDENTS WANT TO LEARN

Questionnaires to determine the interests and goals of the students should be administered not just at the beginning of the term, but on an ongoing basis. This is particularly important in programs with continuous enrollment, as the students attending a class after six weeks may not be the same ones who were surveyed at the beginning of the term. Even in classes in which everyone registers at the same time, students' goals may change over time. Questionnaires can be administered orally or in writing, in the student's first or second language. Box 4 provides an example of a general questionnaire.

At the beginning of a unit it is also helpful to find out what students already know and what they want to know about the new topic. One way to do this is for students individually to fill out an open-ended chart like the one in Box 5 on page 13.

Alternatively, a formal questionnaire on a specific topic can be administered orally or in writing as in the Housing Survey in the Housing unit (Box 60, page 147).

It should be noted that these kinds of preliminary activities actually serve multiple purposes. In addition to the overt purpose of finding out what students know and what they want to know, they also serve to activate schemata (that is, to "awaken" or bring to consciousness existing knowledge) and to focus attention on the new topic.

BOX 4

Needs analysis questionnaire

Put an X in front of each statement which is true for you.

I need to <u>speak</u> and <u>understand</u> more English to:

______ 1. Talk on the telephone	______14. Get a driver's license
______ 2. Talk to my neighbors	______15. Get car insurance
______ 3. Talk to my children	______16. Take care of a traffic ticket
______ 4. Talk to my children's teachers	______17. Talk at the Post Office
______ 5. Watch TV	______18. Give and follow directions
______ 6. Talk to the police	______19. Rent an apartment or house
______ 7. Shop for food	______20. Talk to apartment manager
______ 8. Use money	______21. Shop for clothes
______ 9. Go to a restaurant	______22. Get a job
______10. Talk to a doctor	______23. Apply for job training
______11. Talk to a dentist	______24. Talk at the bank
______12. Buy medicine	______25. Go to university
______13. Take the bus	
______________(your choice)	______________(your choice)

BOX 4 (continued)

I need to <u>read</u> and <u>write</u> more English to:

_____ 1. Read signs	_____ 9. Read traffic laws
_____ 2. Read food labels in a store	_____ 10. Read labels on clothes
_____ 3. Read food ads	_____ 11. Fill out job applications
_____ 4. Read medicine labels	_____ 12. Fill out tax forms
_____ 5. Read the newspaper	_____ 13. Write checks
_____ 6. Read a bus schedule	_____ 14. Read stories to my children
_____ 7. Fill out an application to rent an apartment	_____ 15. Read telephone and electric bills
_____ 8. Read letters	_____ 16. Write compositions for college
_____(your choice)	_____(your choice)

》》→

BOX 5

Topic needs assessment

What I know about _____

What I want to know about _____

What I learned about _____ (to be
completed at the end of the unit)

FINDING OUT ABOUT STUDENTS' LEARNING STYLES AND
STRATEGIES

In addition to collecting information about what to teach, the instructor
needs to find out how to teach a particular group of students. In order
to do this, she will need information about her particular students'
learning styles and strategies. One way to obtain this information is to
ask questions either orally or in questionnaire form. This can be
structured in a jigsaw questionnaire format, in which groups of students
collect information on different topics from all the members of the class.
One of the advantages of this technique is that students are actively
involved in collecting the data and in collating and sharing it in the form
of general statements about the class. For an example, see jigsaw
questionnaire, in the Personal Identification unit (Box 14, page 44).

Possible questions that could be asked concerning learning styles and strategies are given in Box 6. Alternatively, the same questions can be presented in the form of a long questionnaire or several short ones.

Other procedures for eliciting information about students are included throughout the book, but particularly in the units on Building Community in the Classroom and Personal Identification.

BOX 6

Learning styles and strategies questionnaire

Learning mode

Do you like to start with ideas and rules?
Do you like to learn through activities?
Do you like to watch and listen?
Do you learn best when your feelings are involved?

Working alone or with others

Do you like to work alone?
Do you like to work in groups?
Do you like to work in pairs?

Learning new information

Do you like to learn new information by listening to lectures?
Do you like to learn new information by talking with others?
Do you like to learn new information by reading?

Learning new words

Do you remember new words in a foreign language easily?
Do you write new words down to remember them?
Do you make pictures of new words in your mind?
If you come across a new word when you are reading, do you immediately look it up in a dictionary?

What assumptions about language learning underlie this book?

Language is an interrelated and meaningful whole

When we try to separate parts of a language, such as grammar rules from use or vocabulary lists from context, we end up with meaningless bits. Formal aspects of the language should not, in principle, be taught separately from meaning. If we begin with a theme, say clothing, we can integrate vocabulary (items of clothing, colors) and structure (sequence and agreement of adjectives, possessives) into it. Instead of practicing words on a vocabulary list in isolation, students practice new vocabulary by labeling a picture. Later the same words can be dictated and divided by the students into meaningful categories, such as "clothing I wear" and "clothing I don't wear." By presenting structure and vocabulary in meaningful contexts, we can ensure that use reinforces form.

Furthermore, in a holistic view of language, all four skill areas, listening, speaking, reading and writing, are important and support each other. Students talk with each other about a passage they have read or heard and follow up with a writing task on the same topic, thus employing more than one skill. By reusing the same material in a different form, students see that the skills they are learning can be applied in more than one way.

Learning a language is an integrated process

One does not learn a language "brick by brick," mastering one bit before going on to the next. Language learning is a long process, in which the learner gradually increases his ability to understand and express himself, integrating every new bit of learning into an overall competence. This does not mean that learners must wait until they know the past tense of every verb to describe last weekend's activities, or that they cannot attempt to write a journal until they can spell every word they might want to use. It is our belief that students should be encouraged at all levels to use the language at their disposal to communicate with others as best they can. Even in beginning classes, students can participate in activities in which they talk and share information with each other, as in interviews and surveys.

Mistakes are a normal and necessary part of language learning

Indiscriminate correction tends to intimidate learners and discourage communication. Teachers should initially respond to errors that interfere with meaning, such as confusion of he and she or the pronunciation of final "s" on nouns, and ignore errors that do not. As far as possible, students should be given an opportunity to correct themselves. This does not mean that the teacher should never correct, but that the correction should not interfere with or replace the communication of meaning. One strategy is for the teacher to restate correctly, but without making an issue of it, what the student has said. Another way is to collect errors from class members and at some future time look at them together and work out the correct forms. This depersonalizes the correction and separates it from the communicative moment. Similar strategies can be used in writing. In commenting on a student's writing, the teacher can restate what the individual student has written in the form of a comment on the writing as well as collect common errors to be considered at a later time.

The classroom atmosphere affects learning

In a classroom where the atmosphere is friendly and supportive, students are more willing to take risks in using the new language. For any person, but particularly for an adult who finds himself in a new and unfamiliar environment, being recognized and appreciated is extremely important. Perhaps the most crucial role of the teacher is to foster an atmosphere of mutual respect in her class. The teacher's own behavior provides a model. Listening carefully and affirming, giving students time to think and reply, valuing and responding to what each student contributes all demonstrate respect. Showing respect for adult students does not imply letting them behave in whatever ways they choose. Taking turns and listening to others are essential to creating an atmosphere in which everyone can learn. The teacher, as classroom manager, has a responsibility to see that this happens.

The learner is an active partner in the learning process

As an active participant in the learning process, the learner needs to have input into both the content of the course and the way in which it is being taught. He is not just a passive recipient of knowledge. Questionnaires such as those suggested earlier, in the data collection section, provide the teacher with information about the students' interests and needs. At the beginning of a unit, the class can discuss and list what they already know and what they want to know about the new topic. By working as a team, the teacher and students together are better able to explore and customize the teaching program to suit the needs of the learners.

How do you plan a course?

For many language courses there is a predetermined syllabus or coursebook, which teachers are required to follow. This may be a loose outline, specifying what the outcomes of a course are to be, or it may be a day-by-day prescription including specific activities. In other programs there may be little guidance. It may be the teacher's responsibility to plan the course. In that case the teacher must start by determining the basic organizing principles as well as the needs and desires of the students. One way to organize a language course is around grammar points. One unit presents the simple past and another the comparison of adjectives. Situations and language uses (functions) can also be used as organizing principles. Another way to organize a course is to consider the contexts, such as housing and health care, in which the students will need to use the language. Instruction is then organized around themes arising from these contexts. While this book is organized thematically, it also provides access to the activities through the index, which lists specific structures and functions.

Where teachers have the choice, thematic organization has certain advantages. Organizing instruction around themes ensures the learners' interest and motivation because these topics are related directly to their lives. Within each theme the class builds a body of common knowledge, vocabulary, structures, and functions, which provide a sense of security and continuity over time. Gains in fluency and accuracy occur while the students focus on content.

Different themes elicit different functions, vocabulary, and structures, and within a theme these recur, providing an opportunity for recycling material. For example, students may practice the names of parts of the body and then come back to them on different occasions in other ways (such as touching them as they are named, placing cards containing names of body parts in order to make a body on a table or wall, or playing bingo with the words themselves and/or their definitions). Recycling also occurs when the same theme is reintroduced at a higher level and used with more sophisticated structures, vocabulary, and functions. A third way that recycling takes place is across themes. Some material recurs naturally in a variety of contexts: temperatures relate to weather, food, and health; money is part of banking and any kind of shopping; weights and measures occur in food, health, housing, and clothing activities. It is important to watch for these recurrences and point them out to students. It is gratifying to them to see the connections in different language contexts and to recall and reuse what they have learned previously.

Once a teacher has determined which themes are relevant to her class (see Box 5, page 13), she must decide how best to teach them. First, what content, structures, functions, and vocabulary should be included? Second, what is the best sequence for teaching the material? (For example, students need to know words to describe family relationships before making and describing a family tree.) Third, through which activities can the content best be taught? Finally, the teacher must plan individual lessons that include a variety of activities.

What makes a balanced lesson?

A balanced lesson, like a balanced meal, draws elements from various categories. Too many elements from one category make for a class that satisfies some needs but fails to meet others.

Language skills

One part of the balanced "menu" is the basic language skills: speaking, reading, writing, and listening. In planning a class, the instructor should be sure to include activities in each skill area. The class might begin with a dictation, which requires both listening and writing, then go on to an oral pre-reading activity and then to a reading task. By working in several skill areas during each class period, the students improve in those areas in which they need additional work and are able to demonstrate their strengths in others.

Groupings

Another aspect of a balanced lesson plan is grouping: whole class, small groups, pairs, and individuals. Although an entire class period built around pair work might optimize student participation, the students miss out on a sense of class unity. At the same time, if the whole period consists of teacher-fronted, whole-group activities, individual students have little opportunity to interact with each other. A more balanced class might begin with a whole class oral activity, such as a jazz chant, followed by one in which students first generate ideas individually and then share them in a small group.

Difficulty level

Another part of the menu is the "easy" to "hard" continuum. An easier task is characterized by familiarity of materials and task, fewer variables, a clear sequence, and carefully modeled responses, such as a review of the preceding day's reading or questions and answers on a familiar topic. A slightly more difficult activity might require students to use that familiar material for another purpose, such as conducting a survey of classmates. Of course, what may be an easy and comfortable activity for one class or some members of a class might represent a considerable stretch for others. In considering classroom tasks, we should keep in mind that activities that challenge the student to think need not be linguistically difficult. It is important to see that within a given class period, every student is at some points challenged (though not by impossible tasks) and at others is able to demonstrate his strengths comfortably.

Learning modes

Students prefer different learning modes, and the class "menu" should take this into account. In our classes we find it useful to identify the following modes: seeing, hearing, saying, doing, thinking, feeling, and interacting. Most of these modes are self-explanatory, but it should be noted that "seeing" includes not only pictures, charts, and graphs but also written text; "doing" includes any sort of physical activity, such as writing, manipulating objects, and moving around the room; "thinking" consists of analyzing, solving problems, and classifying information; "feeling" denotes an emotional involvement with the material to be learned.

For some students a change of mode can provide a significant challenge. Students can be encouraged to stretch their ways of learning by trying out new modes. At the same time, their preferences should not be ignored.

How to use this chart

A chart such as the one in Box 7 can aid the teacher in planning a balanced lesson, as it provides a simple way to track the range of activities she intends to use. As she plans a lesson, she can list the activities in the left-hand column and fill in the remaining boxes for each activity using the choices in the key. For example, if the activity is one in which the teacher describes the contents of her refrigerator and the students draw it (see page 90), the teacher can fill in "whole class" for groupings, "listening" for language skills, "easy" for difficulty level, and "hearing" and "seeing" for learning modes. Thus she can see at a glance whether her plan includes activities with different groupings, language skills, difficulty levels, and learning modes. The chart can also be used following a class as a tool for reflecting upon one's classroom practice.

BOX 7

Lesson menu chart

Activity	Groupings	Language skills	Difficulty level	Learning modes

Key:

Groupings	Language Skills	Difficulty	Learning Modes
Whole class	Reading	Easy	Seeing
Small groups	Writing	Medium	Hearing
Pairs	Listening	Hard	Saying
Individuals	Speaking		Doing
			Thinking
			Feeling
			Interacting

How can a teacher work with a multilevel class?

Every second language class is in some sense multilevel in terms of language skills. Some students read and write better than their classmates; others are more proficient at speaking or listening. Some know grammar rules backward and forward but are unable to speak. Some classes are multilevel because only one level is offered at a particular time or place. Even those classes that begin fairly homogeneously become multilevel as students progress at differing rates.

How then should a multilevel class be taught? One solution is to aim for the middle. There are times when all teachers do this. Clearly, however, it is a disservice to those on either side of the middle if the entire class is conducted in this way. Those at the higher levels are bored and those at the lower levels have little chance for success. At the other extreme is the option of creating individualized packets of materials for each student, tailored for his or her level. Most teachers are not willing or able to do this. In addition, a disadvantage of totally individualized work is that communication among students is minimized.

It is possible, however, to organize a class around activities in which all students can participate and to which they can contribute at their own levels. This does not preclude using parts of the class period to have students work on materials geared specifically to their level, but it means that during much of the class there are shared activities across levels.

In any activity, there are three elements: materials or input, task, and performance level. Materials and input include any information that is given to the student as a basis for the activity. This might include written text, pictures, charts, and instructions. The task is what the student actually does with that input, such as asking a partner questions or writing down information from a dictation. Performance level is a reflection of proficiency: that is, lower level students perform using simpler vocabulary and structures. They may rely on a partner to read or write for them. Higher level students are expected to demonstrate more sophisticated use of language. We can vary the level of an activity by modifying any of these elements. The four types of activities that follow can be used effectively in multilevel classes as well as in more homogeneous ones. Most of the activities in this book fall within these four types.

Same input/same task

In the first type of activity, all students are given the same input and are assigned the same task. The input may be in the form of pictures, puzzles, charts, graphs, or simply stated problems. The input is in some way challenging or interesting, and understanding it requires drawing on previous knowledge and experience. The first-aid problems in the unit on health (page 167) are an example of this type of activity. Some who are skilled language learners may be less skilled at resolving challenges of this sort, whereas others, because of their particular backgrounds and experiences, may be very good at them regardless of their language proficiency. Working cooperatively in pairs or groups, students are able to make the most of their particular talents.

Same input/modified task

The second type of activity differs from the first in that although the input remains the same, the tasks are modified by the teacher according to the students' levels. One example of this is a multilevel dictation. All students hear the same dictation (input), but higher-proficiency students are expected to write the entire dictation without written cues. Lower-level students write only numbers or familiar words. An example of this can be seen on page 55 in the unit on family. Activities of this type reduce the frustration of lower level students by making the task one they can complete successfully, while not depriving higher level students of a greater challenge. At the same time, the whole class is working on the same basic material.

Different input/same task

In the third type of activity, all students are given the same task, but the input is modified according to their level. For example, in a "find someone who" kind of activity, lower-level students are given ready-made questions, while their more proficient classmates are given cues from which they must formulate their own questions. All the students participate together in identifying classmates who fit their descriptions. This activity is described in detail in the unit on building community in the classroom (page 30).

Same task/different performance level

The fourth category includes those activities for which the teacher does not actually give the students materials, but just sets the task. One task might be to produce a class cookbook (page 108). Students draw on their own backgrounds and experience as well as their knowledge of English to contribute to this task. As another example, students make a family tree (page 62) and share it with a partner. The language produced by the students in carrying out this sort of task will vary according to their level.

How do you choose teaching materials?

Whether you use one basic textbook or put together your own package of class materials, there are many factors to consider when choosing teaching materials. The first consideration is whether the materials are appropriate to the students and the course. For instance, although children's books may be easy to read, many adults feel insulted and diminished by being asked to use them. A book intended for people who plan to visit the country as tourists is not appropriate for those who are immigrants. If you are teaching a theme-based course, a book organized around grammatical structures will not be suitable.

It is important to look carefully at the content of the materials. Is the language real? Does it reflect what people actually say and hear, read and write? Are the pictures, stories, and situations relevant and interesting to your students? It is hard for a student in a small town in Missouri to become involved with situations that involve subways or maps of New York City. Do stories or dialogues carry their own meaning, or are they simply vehicles for grammatical structures or vocabulary lists?

At the same time, it is important to look at textbook exercises to be sure that they do not just ask obvious questions, but that they also require the student to reflect on what he has read. There should be challenging and interesting exercises that require students to think and apply what they have learned.

How is the rest of this book organized?

An important starting point for any language class is building community in the classroom. Accordingly, the next section is about initial and ongoing activities and grouping strategies to help the class gain a sense of solidarity, inclusion, and comfort, which is essential to free and easy communication.

The theme-based units in this book describe specific classroom activities organized around topics that are common to adult second language programs: personal identification, family, community, food, clothing, housing, health, work, and money. Each activity includes a title and brief description, information about how long the activity takes, levels for which it is appropriate, the main teaching points, how students are grouped, preparation required, and the procedure to be followed. In addition, many of the activities include suggested follow-ups to extend the activity and variations to accommodate different student levels. The book concludes with an annotated bibliography of useful books in the field and an index.

Building community in the classroom

One of the surest ways to get students to use their new language is by building a sense of community in the classroom. Students who feel that they are part of a classroom community want to talk to each other, to tell about themselves and their lives, and in turn to learn more about their classmates. The resulting communication not only helps a class run more smoothly, it increases the students' commitment to learning the new language and to forming relationships in it. Furthermore, because the focus of their communication is on what they want to say and not on how they say it, students feel more at ease speaking their new language and are consequently more willing to take the risks involved in using a second language. In this section, we consider strategies and techniques the teacher can use to foster a sense of community in her class.

Arranging the classroom

Many adult classes take place in borrowed spaces, in schools, community buildings, or churches. While some of these places lend themselves to adult classes without modification, in other cases the teacher may need to adapt the space to the needs of her class. The way that classroom seats are arranged can go a long way toward encouraging communication. Many teachers are faced with immovable seats or other spatial limitations and must work within those constraints. However, those who can move seats find that students communicate more with each other when they are able to see the faces (rather than the backs) of their classmates. Arranging seats in a large circle or semicircle or in rows facing each other increases communication. Moving seats at the beginning of class and moving them back at the end may seem like a lot of work, but most teachers find their students more than willing to help and the results well worth the effort.

The size and arrangement of class space can also make it difficult to have communicative activities that require learners to move around. If there is furniture in the way, students can be asked to help move it to one side and later replace it. Alternatively, hallways or other large spaces in a building can be utilized for such activities.

Students and teachers like to feel that the space in which they meet belongs to them, if only for the time during which they meet. Displaying photographs of students and class activities and of work done in class contributes to that feeling. Such materials can be displayed on classroom or hallway walls. In borrowed space, the teacher can attach them to easily moved pieces of cardboard or long strings that can be quickly put up and taken down.

Establishing classroom routines

Classroom routines lend predictability to a class. Members of a class feel more comfortable with their teacher as well as with their classmates when they know what to expect. At the most basic level, these include routines for starting and ending the class.

Starting class

A routine for starting class is beneficial because it signals to all of the students that it is time to be seated and start to work. The following are some possible routines for the beginning of class:

1. Greet individual students and ask a question: What did you do last night? What are you going to do this weekend? What did you do during the weekend? The question might be linked to the current unit: Did you take the bus or drive this morning? What's the weather forecast for today? What was on TV last night?
2. Review the preceding class, a particularly valuable activity in classes where students do not attend every session.
3. Assign one student each day to take class "minutes" and read them aloud at the beginning of the next class.
4. Write on the board, post a sheet of paper, or use an overhead transparency to give a preview of the day's activities. The preview can be revisited at the end of class so that students can see what they have accomplished.
5. Begin each class with a writing assignment. The teacher might write a sentence or the beginning of a sentence on a large poster and have the students comment on it or complete it. A writing topic related to the preceding day's work or previewing upcoming work can be posted for students to begin when they arrive.
6. Begin with a dictation on the current unit of study. Easily available popular reference books such as *The World Almanac*, newspapers, or magazines provide information that lends itself to dictation. For example, for a unit on food, read the names of specific foods and the

number of calories per serving of each; when studying health, read a list of suggestions for preventing colds.

Ending class

Just as starting routines are useful, so are ending routines. The following are examples of such activities:

1. Summarize the day's lesson.
2. Review with the students the preview sheet from the beginning of class.
3. Have students contribute orally or in writing to a group summary.
4. Ask students in turn to write on the board or a large sheet of paper a new word or concept they learned that day.
5. Preview the next lesson.
6. Have the students write for one minute on the least understood point of the day's lesson or on how they can use what they learned in class that day.

Pair and group work

Working together in groups helps students feel that they are part of a community. They come to know each other as individuals and as friends. Because adult students come with widely differing skills and backgrounds, it is important that they all have the opportunity to participate together in their learning. Pair and group work also serves an important pedagogical purpose because it provides more opportunities for individuals to talk than does a teacher-fronted class, as well as a less formal and potentially threatening environment.

Factors involved in forming groups

Groups can be formed in a variety of ways, depending on the purpose of the group work. Always putting the same students together may be convenient, but it reduces the contacts they have with other classmates as well as their sense of unity with the entire group. Furthermore, because the same students do not necessarily attend every session of a class, it is very difficult to count on having the same groups from session to session of adult classes. Levels of proficiency may be important when organizing groups for some purposes, such as combining students at the same level for a task pitched specifically to that level or intentionally combining students at different levels so that the higher-level students can assist the lower-level ones while at the same time strengthening their own communication skills. There may also be other considerations in grouping, such as avoiding a concentration of students from one language group or of a single age or gender.

Techniques for forming groups

1. Assign groups according to where students sit. This is the simplest and quickest way to group students, but it has the disadvantage that many people tend to sit next to friends who share their first language. If the purpose of the activity is to have students share their cultures, for example, this is not a satisfactory way to group them.
2. Count off the students, giving each person a number up to the number of groups you want, and then starting over (1, 2, 3, 1, 2, 3). Then have all the 1s sit together, all the 2s, and so on. This is an easy way to form groups, but because people often sit in the same seats, they may end up working with the same group each time.
3. Have the students draw numbers from an envelope and find the person or people with the matching number by saying the number aloud. Numbers with similar pronunciation can be used, so that, for example, the students must pronounce the number 14 carefully in order not to confuse it with 40. This gives the students a chance to practice pronunciation and aural discrimination as they are forming groups. Letters of the alphabet may be used in the same way.
4. Provide slips of paper with group designations such as pictures or words related to the topic being studied. For example, in a unit on clothing, one group might have the designation "shoe" and another "glove." Put the papers in an envelope and have each student choose one and then find others with the same designation to form a group. A more difficult version requires students to put together "families": shoes, boots, sandals in one group; shirt, jacket, sweater in another. Students review vocabulary at the same time they find members of their group.
5. Cut pictures into several pieces. Tell students to find those who have parts of the same picture by walking around the room and describing what is in their part of the picture.
6. Tell students to line up by one of the following: favorite number, age (including an "I'd rather not say" category for those who prefer not to tell), shoe size, birthday, how long they have been in the country, how long they have studied their second language, how long they have been married, how long it takes them to get to class, how much change they have in their pockets, what time they get up in the morning, or any other category that is relevant to class work. Once they are in line, they can be divided into groups.
7. At times you may want students divided into several sequential

groups for jigsaw or other activities. In other words, students first meet in one group to tell a story, share information, or interpret a common text. They then take their story or information or text to a second group of people who are unfamiliar with their material. One way to divide students sequentially, if the students are only going to regroup once, is to set up the first group by assigning numbers or letters (the text itself can have a designating letter on it) to each group. Then, as the groups are concluding the first part of the task, assign each member a second designation, for example, a 1, 2, or 3 or an A, B, or C or a bird, a butterfly, or a tiger. The students then join the new group.

8. It is more complicated when you want to have a third regrouping that does not replicate the previous ones. For example, if each student is to tell a joke or share a picture and you want each student to do the same thing several times, you want a new audience for each telling. Box 8 shows a scheme that can be used for such grouping. Give each student a slip of paper with the vertical designations on it. The first A will be a 1 for the second grouping and a flower for the third. The second will first be an A, then a 2, and finally a turtle. In cases where the student numbers do not divide evenly into groups, two students may be given the same designation.

BOX 8

Grouping scheme

A	A	A	B	B	B
1	2	3	1	2	3
C	C	C	D	D	D
1	2	3	1	2	3
E	E	E			
1	2	3			

Copyright © Cambridge University Press.

Getting acquainted

Obviously, introduction and name-learning activities are used at the beginning of the term. However, in many adult classes with open entry policies, new students enter classes throughout the term. Consequently, activities of this type should be repeated from time to time so that new students feel they belong in the class and so that continuing students include them in the community. Here are some suggestions for making introductions in class.

1. Ask each student to introduce himself to the class. Those with more limited language skills may choose to make quite formulaic self-introductions, modeled by the teacher, perhaps including only name and country. Others may choose to expand their introductions

by telling one or two things about themselves. From time to time, stop the introductions and ask the rest of the class to review the names and other information they have just heard.

2. Have each student in turn teach the other students how to say his name correctly. The students may at the same time write their names on the board and show their classmates on a map the location of their native country and city.

3. Give each student a half-piece of paper and a marker. Give the following instructions:

   (a) Fold the paper in half horizontally so that it can be placed on the table or desk as a name card.
   (b) Put your name on the paper so that others can read it easily.
   (c) In each corner of the paper, write a word, a picture, or a number that relates to you.

   Have each student interview a neighboring student in order to learn more about the cues on the paper and to introduce him to the class. The cards can later be propped up on the table or desk in front of the students in order to help students (and the teacher) learn each others' names. The teacher may then dictate the spelling of each person's name and have the students identify who it is. The teacher may also make statements (such as "She likes cats") or questions ("Who has a new car?") about an item from a student's name card and have the others identify who it is. Students can also make statements about each other based on those items.

4. For this activity you will need a ball of yarn. Ask the students to stand in a circle and model both self-introductions (My name is . . . or I am . . .) and throwing the yarn to a student in the circle while holding onto the end of the yarn. Give the yarn to the first student. He introduces himself and throws the ball of yarn to another student but holds onto the end of it. The next student also introduces himself and passes on the yarn but continues to hold onto a bit of it. This continues until all the students are linked by the yarn. Reverse the process, but as the students undo the yarn, have each person say the name of the person to whom he is passing the yarn.

5. The "find someone who" kind of exercise provides opportunities for practicing question asking and can be tailored to class level and topic. Each student is given a list of questions and must walk around the room until he finds and gets the signature of a classmate who can answer yes to each question. For lower-level students, provide the questions. Higher-level students can make up their own questions from prompts. Some possible items are listed in Box 9.

6. In an intermediate or advanced class, ask students to write a letter introducing themselves to the class. The teacher may also write one. Tell each student to pass his completed letter to the person on his right. As that person reads the letter, he adds comments or questions about its contents. Continue passing the letters around until everyone has read and commented on each letter. Then ask the class to tell what they have learned about each student. The author of the letter can answer any questions or respond to comments. Students in larger classes can be divided into groups of eight to ten for this activity. The letters make a nice record of early writing.

7. As students introduce themselves to visitors or to new classmates, vary the routine by having them introduce a classmate and tell something about him. Have each student write his name on a small piece of paper and put the papers in an envelope or a paper bag. As each person draws a name, he introduces that person.

In the remainder of this book you will find many more activities through which the classroom community can be strengthened and supported through sharing and cooperative work.

BOX 9

Find someone who . . .

1. is from Russia
2. is looking for a job
3. has one child
4. has a driver's license
5. likes the color blue
6. is from Japan
7. does not have a driver's license
8. plans to stay here one year
9. likes cold weather
10. is from China
11. likes hot weather
12. likes the color red
13. takes the bus to class
14. is more than thirty years old
15. has two children

Theme-based units

Personal identification

Personal identification is a good starting point for a new class. It gives students an opportunity to get to know each other and to share personal information, which they know well. Thus students begin their language study with a sense of self-confidence. As they share personal information with classmates, they learn what they have in common, which often leads to further conversation and friendship. They will practice using numbers and spelling words out loud. As students fill out job applications and other forms, they need to know how to read them and provide the appropriate information.

In talking about their own personal information, students need to use the pronoun I and first person verb forms. When telling about a classmate, they must distinguish masculine and feminine pronouns as well as third person verb forms.

Treasured object

Students share with their classmates objects that have special significance for them.

Time: 30 to 40 minutes
Level: Beginning and up
Main teaching points: Share personal information
                               Use past tenses
                               Use possessives
Organization: Groups of three or four students
Preparation: Ask the students in advance to bring into class an object with special significance for them. Bring an object of your own so that you can model what you want the students to do.

Procedure

1. Show the object you have brought. Tell the class why it has special meaning for you.
2. Brainstorm with the students and write on the board vocabulary they may need for describing their objects. Also brainstorm a list of questions and comments that listeners might want to use.

3. Divide the students into groups of three or four and give each student a few minutes to explain to his group why the object has special meaning for him. If any student is without an object, he can draw the object and/or describe it before talking about it.
3. Regroup the students (see page 27) and have them tell the new group about their objects.
4. Bring the whole class together and ask them to share what they have learned about their classmates.

Variation: Whole-class presentations may be substituted for group presentations.
Follow-up: The students can write about their objects and include them in a class treasure book.

Personal time lines

Students plot significant events in their lives on a time line and discuss them with a partner.

Time: 40 minutes
Level: Beginning and up
Main teaching points: Describe events in chronological order
                        Use past tenses
Organization: Individuals, pairs, whole class
Preparation: Prepare a time line of your own life on a large sheet of paper. An example is given in Box 10.

Procedure

1. Have the students brainstorm a list of important events in their lives, such as birth, beginning and end of school, moving, marriage, birth of a child, war, sickness. Write key words on the blackboard.
2. Show the students your own time line and talk through the events.
3. Ask the students to think about important events in their own lives and to draw a time line showing these events. They may use pictures, symbols, or words, or a combination of all three.
4. As students finish, put them together in pairs to discuss their pictures. Ask them to change partners until each student has explained his time line to at least two other students.

Follow-up: Post a very long piece of paper on the wall with dates at ten-year intervals (1940, 1950, etc.). Ask each student to record three to five events from his life on the time line. Use the large time line as a basis for question-and-answer practice (for example, "Who was born in 1961?").

BOX 10

Sample time line

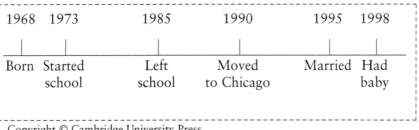

1968	1973	1985	1990	1995	1998
Born	Started school	Left school	Moved to Chicago	Married	Had baby

Sentence starters

Students complete sentence starters and then introduce each other to the class on the basis of this information.

Time: 30 to 40 minutes
Level: Beginning and up
Main teaching points: Share personal information
Introduce someone
Complete sentences
Subject-verb agreement
Organization: Individuals, pairs, whole class
Preparation: None

Procedure

1. Write the following on the board, one beneath the other: My name is . . . , I speak . . . , I am . . . , I have . . . , I like . . . , I want . . . , I need. The number and degree of difficulty of these "sentence starters" can be varied according to the level of the students and, of course, responses will vary according to level.
2. Ask the students to complete each sentence on a piece of paper.
3. Pair students and ask them to use the information on the paper to introduce their partners to the class.

Variation: Collect and redistribute the papers and have each person find the person whose paper he has and introduce him to the class.
Follow-up: Ask students to walk around the room with their own papers looking for classmates who have the same answer as they have for one or more of the questions.

BOX 11

Personal information grid

Name	Address	Phone	Country	Language

Tell me about you

Students gather personal information about their classmates.

Time: 30 minutes
Level: Beginning and up
Main teaching points: Ask for and give personal information
　　　　　　　　　　　　　　Use question forms
Organization: Pairs, whole class
Preparation: You will need to make a model grid with the following categories across the top (see Box 11): *Phone number, Address, Language, Country,* and, if desired, other information such as *Married/single, Children/no children, Occupation.* If you want the students to practice spelling their names orally, you might put only first names and have last names as a separate category.

Procedure

1. Post the model grid on the wall or board. Have the students copy the grid, including the names of the students who are in class. The names can be listed on the grid or, if all of the students are able to understand, students can dictate their own names, spelling them.
2. When all of the students have copied the grid, review the questions they will need to ask their classmates in order to fill in the information. Sample questions can be left on the board to provide cues for students as they fill in their grids.
3. Tell the students to walk around the class and interview their

classmates to get the information they need to fill in the grid. Walk around during the activity, checking to be sure the information is being conveyed orally and in English. Encourage students to spell words if necessary and to ask for repetition when they do not understand an answer.
4. Bring the class together. Fill in the large grid by having students dictate the answers to other students or to the teacher or by having the students write in the answers directly.

Variations

1. In a very large class, the students can be divided into groups, with each group responsible only for its own members and a separate model sheet for each group.
2. Lower-level students might be asked to complete only the telephone and address part of the grid.

Follow-ups

1. The grid can be kept on the wall for a few days, and students can return to it for question-and-answer practice.
2. Have students construct other information grids on likes, dislikes, interests, habits, and so on.

Personal information form

Students first match questions and answers and then complete a personal information form.

Time: 40 minutes
Level: Beginning to intermediate
Main teaching points: Ask for and give personal information
                            Use question forms
Organization: Whole class and pairs
Preparation: Prepare enough cut-up sentence strips (Box 12 on page 41) so that each student receives one. Prepare one copy of the personal information form (Box 13 on page 42) for each student.

Procedure

1. Give each student a sentence strip. The object of the activity is to find the person who holds the other half of the question and answer. As they walk around the room, those with questions look for the corresponding answer and those with answers look for the matching question. This should be done orally, students reading their questions aloud.
2. When they have found their partners, ask them to sit down together.

3. Have the pairs read their questions and answers to the whole class. Discuss any mismatches.
4. Hand out copies of the personal information form and have the students take turns asking questions and completing as much as they can in 10 minutes using information from their partners.
5. If students have not completed all the items on the form in the time allocated, they may take their own forms home and complete them.

Variation

1. Go through the questions first with the students and decide what kind of answers to look for.
2. Have each student draw a strip from an envelope.
3. While the students remain in their seats, one person with a question asks it, and the person who has the answer responds. The students may use the personal information form as a guide to sequence.
4. Repeat until all the questions have been asked.

BOX 12

Sentence strips

What is your name?	Maria Sanchez
Where do you live?	16 Browning Avenue Arlington, Virginia
What is your telephone number?	555-8694
Are you married or single?	Married
Do you have any children?	Yes, two daughters and one son
Do you have relatives in the United States?	Yes, my mother and my sister live here
What country do you come from?	Mexico
How old are you?	34
When were you born?	August 15, 1963
What languages do you speak?	Spanish and English
How long have you been living in the United States?	I've been here for 5 months

BOX 13

Personal information form

What is your name?	
Where do you live?	
What is your telephone number?	
Are you married or single?	
Do you have any children?	
Do you have relatives in the United States?	
What country do you come from?	
How old are you?	
When were you born?	
What languages do you speak?	
How long have you been living in the United States?	

Jigsaw questionnaire

Students collect and collate personal information about their classmates.

Time: 30 to 40 minutes
Level: Beginning and up
Main teaching points: Make generalizations
　　　　　　　　Ask and answer questions in the simple present,
　　　　　　　　simple past, and present perfect
Organization: Same-level groups
　　　　　　　Mixed-level groups
　　　　　　　Whole class
Preparation: Prepare sets of questions for each group (see Box 14).
　Group 1 gets the questions designated group 1, and so on. Make
　enough copies so that each person in the group has one and there are
　several spare copies. Each group of four students will need a large
　sheet of paper and a marker.

Procedure

1. Divide the students into four groups of roughly equal size.
2. Give one set of questions to each group. Ask the students to read
   through and discuss the questions together but *not* to answer
   them. Walk around and be ready to clarify any questions at this
   time.
3. Regroup the students, so that their new groups include someone
   from each of the original groups.
4. Tell the students to take turns asking and recording the answers to
   the questions on their sheet. They will need to record the number of
   yes answers and the number of *no* answers. Remind them to include
   their own answers when they are asking the questions.
5. When the groups have finished, ask them to return to their original
   groups. Give each group a large piece of paper and a marker. On
   the paper they are to (a) record the answers they got for the whole
   class and (b) prepare some general statements about the class based
   on these figures – for example, most of the people in this class are
   married.
6. Have each group present their findings to the whole class.

Variations

1. The questionnaires are in order of increasing difficulty, so you
   may choose to group students based on language level and give a
   level-specific group of questions to each group.
2. For higher-level learners, more difficult questions may be
   substituted.

⋙➤

43

BOX 14

Jigsaw questionnaire

Group 1		
	Yes	**No**
Are you married?		
Do you have children?		
Do you live alone?		

Group 2		
	Yes	**No**
Do you have a middle name?		
Are you older than 40?		
Are you younger than 25?		

Group 3		
	Yes	**No**
Did you study ——————— (L2) in your country?		
Did you have a job in your country?		
Do you have a job now?		

BOX 14 (continued)

Group 4

	Yes	No
Have you been in this country more than 6 months?		
Have you been in this country less than 3 months?		
Have you ever lived in a foreign country before?		

Interviews

Students interview each other and their teacher.

Time: 40 to 60 minutes
Level: High beginners and up
Main teaching points: Share personal information
Ask and answer questions
Use pronouns
Organization: Whole class and pairs
Preparation: None

Procedure

1. Tell the students that they are going to interview you, the teacher. Ask each student to write on the board one question he would like you to answer. Each student should write a different question.
2. When all the questions are on the board, have the students check them first for duplicates and second for grammar.
3. Answer the questions as fully as possible.
4. Tell the students that they are going to interview one of their classmates. Ask them to identify questions on the board that would not be appropriate to ask and to add any additional questions that they could ask their partners.

5. Pair the students and give them 10 minutes each to interview their partner.
6. After they have finished, have the students tell the class what they have learned about their partners.

Variation: Students who are not yet literate can make a tape that can then serve as a dictation for a higher-level student.

Follow-up: Have the students write each others' stories and then post them on the wall. Give partners a chance to review the stories and make alterations before posting. This is a good way to introduce the peer review process, as students care very much what is written and "published" about them.

Find your identical twin

Students must find another student in the class who has a matching set of personal information.

Time: 20 minutes
Level: High beginners and up
Main teaching points: Share personal information
                         Ask and answer questions
Organization: Pairs, whole class
Preparation: You will need to select the cue cards that you wish to use from Box 15 and then make two copies of each. Each student should have one card. You may select and distribute cards according to the level of the students; for example, Level 1 cards can be given to lower-level students. However, it is essential that the twin card is also distributed.

Procedure

1. Give each student a card. Tell him that another student has a card which is exactly the same.
2. Have the students walk around the room to find the person in the class who has the identical card. They may not look at their classmates' cards but may ask and answer questions. Warn them that many of the cards are similar, but their job is to find their *exact* twin.
3. When they have found their exact twin, they should sit down together and try to discover as many things as possible that they have in common in real life.
4. Have the students share with the class the things they have in common.

Follow-up: Students can make their own sets of "twin cards" to be used in another class.

BOX 15

Identical twins cue cards

Level 1

My name is Mary. My telephone number is 555-9683. I live in London. I am married.	My name is Mary. My telephone number is 555-9683. I live in London. I am single.
My name is Mary. My telephone number is 555-9682. I live in London. I am single.	My name is Edin. My telephone number is 555-9683. I live in London. I am single.
My name is Edin. My telephone number is 555-9683. I live in Chicago. I am married.	My name is Edin. My telephone number is 555-9683. I live in Chicago. I am single.

Level 2

My name is Alex. My telephone number is 555-6254. I live in Lagos. I am single. I am 30. I speak English and Spanish.	My name is Alex. My telephone number is 555-6254. I live in Lagos. I am married. I am 30. I speak English and Spanish.
My name is Alex. My telephone number is 555-6254. I live in Lagos. I am single. I am 13. I speak English and Spanish.	My name is Alex. My telephone number is 555-6254. I live in Lagos. I am single. I am 30. I speak English, Spanish, and Portuguese.

⤖→

BOX 15 (continued)

Level 3

My name is Rasema.
My telephone number is
  555-2379.
I live in Paris.
I am married.
I am 37.
I have two children.
I was born in Poland.
I speak French and Spanish.
I have been in France for 8
  months.
	My name is Rasema.
	My telephone number is
	  555-2379.
	I live in Paris.
	I am married.
	I am 37.
	I don't have any children.
	I was born in Poland.
	I speak French and Spanish.
	I have been in France for 8
	  months.

My name is Rasema.
My telephone number is
  555-2379.
I live in Paris.
I am married.
I am 37.
I don't have any children.
I was born in Poland.
I speak French and Spanish.
I have been in France for 2
  years.
	My name is Rasema.
	My telephone number is
	  555-2379.
	I live in Paris.
	I am married.
	I am 37.
	I don't have any children.
	I was born in Poland.
	I speak French and Chinese.
	I have been in France for 2
	  years.

What roles do I play?

Students examine and discuss the roles they play in their own lives.

Time: 30 to 40 minutes
Level: High beginning to intermediate
Main teaching points: Reflect on personal roles
Rank items
Make comparisons
Organization: Whole class, individuals, small groups
Preparation: None

Procedure

1. Have the class brainstorm the various roles they play in their lives, such as mother, cook, worker. Write these on the board. Ask the students to think about which of their roles are more important to them than others.
2. Ask the students to write down all their roles and to represent the importance of each role by the size of the letters they use (see Box 16).
3. Have them compare their papers in small groups, finding similarities and differences. Some of these can be shared with the whole class.

Follow-up: Students can write about themselves using the role vocabulary they have been practicing.

BOX 16

Roles diagram

father

husband

son

worker

Cultural questionnaire

Students explore differences between cultures related to personal identification.

Time: 20 to 30 minutes
Level: Intermediate
Main teaching points: Identify differences between cultures regarding personal information
Use multiple-choice format
Consider different points of view
Organization: Individuals, small groups, whole class
Preparation: Prepare a copy of the questionnaire (Box 17) for each student.

Procedure

1. Give each student a copy of the questionnaire and ask him to complete it from the point of view of his own culture.
2. When all the students have done this, ask them to compare their answers in groups. As far as possible, try to have students from a variety of cultures in each group.
3. Ask the groups what differences they have found.
4. Ask the groups to decide how a person from the host culture would answer these questions.
5. Discuss with the whole class.

Follow-ups

1. Have the students in groups find and discuss more differences between their cultures regarding personal identification customs.
2. Have the students brainstorm what they would like to know about personal identification customs in the country in which they are living. Then have groups of students investigate and report back to the class.

Note: This activity is not appropriate for a class in which all the students come from the same cultural background.

BOX 17

Cross-cultural personal identification questionnaire

1. How do you say your name?

   a. Family name first _____

   b. Your name first _____

   c. Other _____

2. Do you have the same family name as

   a. Your father _____

   b. Your mother _____

   c. Your husband or wife _____

   d. Other _____

3. How do you count your age?

   a. When you are born, you are one _____

   b. One year after you are born, you are one _____

   c. Other_____

4. When someone asks who or what you are, do you talk about

   a. Your family _____

   b. Your appearance _____

   c. Your age in relation to others _____

   d. Other _____

⟫→

BOX 17 (continued)

5. When you describe your appearance, do you tell about

    a. Height and weight _____

    b. Eye and hair color _____

    c. Skin color _____

    d. Face and eye shape _____

    e. Other _____

6. When you write your date of birth, do you

    a. Put the month first and then the day and year

       (11/15/50) _____

    b. Put the day first and then the month and the year

       (15/11/50) _____

    c. Other _____

Emergency phone calls

Students work in pairs and select the best way to continue a dialogue from among alternatives provided. The dialogue focuses on giving personal information in an emergency situation.

Time: 15 minutes
Level: Intermediate
Main teaching points: Ask for emergency assistance
                         Provide personal information
Organization: Pairs, whole class
Preparation: Make copies of dialogue sheet A for half the class and of dialogue sheet B for the other half (Box 18).

Procedure

1. Divide the students into pairs. Give one partner sheet A and the other sheet B. Direct the students not to look at their partners' papers.
2. Explain that they each have half of a dialogue and that their job is to read the dialogue together. The first sentence is given, but after that they must select from two choices the one that fits best in the dialogue. This means that they must listen carefully to their partner's sentence before making their own selection.
3. Ask the students to read through the dialogue together, making appropriate choices.
4. Have several pairs read the dialogue aloud to the class. Discuss why alternative selections do not work.

Variation: Shorter versions of the dialogue may be given to lower-level students.
Follow-up: Have students construct their own dialogues.

BOX 18

Emergency dialogue

SHEET A	SHEET B
1. This is 911. What emergency service do you need?	2. a. Ambulance please, my husband fell off a ladder. b. My name is Linda Turner.
3. a. Are you hurt badly? b. Is he conscious?	4. a. Yes but he can't move his leg. b. He was painting the window.
5. a. Do you have any children? b. Give me your name and telephone number.	6. a. Linda Turner and my number is 555-6542. b. 13 Villawood Boulevard.
7. a. What is your address? b. It's nice to meet you.	8. a. His name is Tom Turner. b. 13 Villawood Boulevard, Webster Grove.
9. a. OK. I'll send an ambulance right away. b. Just leave him; he'll be OK.	10. a. Please hurry; he's in a lot of pain. b. I'll make an appointment for Monday.

Family

Family is a topic to which everyone can contribute something. Students learn or review how to give personal information relating to members of the family: names, ages, birthdates, addresses, phone numbers. Structures include the correct forms for names, ages, and dates; possessives; subject pronouns; and subject-verb agreement. Brochures on activities for children, school announcements and newsletters, and sample school enrollment forms are useful reading materials for parents. Students can find common ground through sharing photographs and family trees.

Family dictation

Students write a dictation about the teacher's family.

Time: 20 minutes
Level: Beginning to intermediate
Main teaching points: Write from dictation
                         Ask for repetition
Organization: Individuals, pairs
Preparation: This activity is most effective and authentic if you use your own family for the dictation. Prepare the dictation based on your family, using the model in Box 19. Parents or siblings can be used rather than children. The model provided is suited to lower-level classes. In writing your own dictation, use structures and vocabulary appropriate to the level of your class.

Procedure

1. Each student will need a piece of paper to record the dictation. Instruct the students to listen and write what they hear, not to check with the person next to them. Encourage them to ask for repetition if they need it.
2. Read the passage at a normal rate, dividing the sentences into meaningful chunks – for example, "His birthday is . . . April 20" – and pause briefly after each chunk. Repeat chunks as needed. After

the first reading, allow students time to read what they have written. Then read it again so that they can check their writing and fill in any gaps.

3. Reread the dictation and then have students check their work in pairs or by comparing it to posted versions. Time should be allowed for them to ask questions about your family.

Variations

1. In a beginning class, write the dictation for students to copy, leaving blanks for numbers and other familiar words (Box 19).
2. In a mixed-level class, use two overheads or large sheets of paper, one with the most of the text for beginning students and the other with more blanks for middle-level students (Box 19). Have the students face in the direction of the one appropriate to their level.

Follow-up: Each student can write about his or her family. Beginning students may follow the pattern supplied by the dictation, including information about their own families. More advanced students may expand on the model or write in any way they choose. These passages can in turn be used for pair dictation.

BOX 19

Dictation

Model dictation (in full):

I have 2 sons. My older son's name is Michael. He is 26 years old. His birthday is June 4th. He lives in Africa. My younger son's name is Jason. He is 23 years old. His birthday is April 20th. He lives in Kansas.

Dictation 1

I have _____ sons. My older son's name is Michael. He is _____ years old. His birthday is June _____ th. He lives in Africa. My younger son's name is Jason. He is _____ years old. His birthday is April _____ th. He lives in Kansas.

Dictation 2

I have _____ sons. My older son's _____ is Michael. He is _____ years _____. His birthday _____ June _____ th. He lives _____ Africa. My younger _____ name is Jason. _____ is _____ years old. His _____ is April _____ th. He _____ in Kansas.

Dictation 3

Students write the entire passage without written cues.

Family strips

Students use their knowledge of family relationships in order to understand sentences.

Version 1

The sentences in Box 20 are written on large strips of paper, which can be taped to the wall or given to individual students or pairs of students.

Time: 20 minutes
Level: Beginning to intermediate
Main teaching points: Solve problems using knowledge of family
        relationships
        Use family vocabulary
        Understand possessives
Organization: Pairs, groups, whole class
Preparation: Prepare large strips of paper with the sentences in Box 20
  on them.

Procedure

1. Post the strips and ask the students to decide which are true, which are false, and which are possibly true or possibly false. Explain to the students that some items may not fit easily into these categories.
2. Designate individuals to move the strips so that the statements are gathered into three groups: true, false, and possibly true or possibly false.

Variation: Copy the sentences on paper, one set for each group of two or three students. Cut them up and clip each set together. Then give them to the students to sort into the categories listed in step 1.
Follow-up: Higher-level students can make up their own family sentences and try them out on their classmates. Lower-level students can copy the false ones, changing them so that they are true.

BOX 20

Family strips

My mother's sister is my aunt.

My father's brother is my son.

My grandmother's daughter is my sister.

My mother is my sister's mother.

My wife's father is my grandfather.

My son's aunt is my sister.

My child's grandmother is my mother.

My sister's daughter is my niece.

My uncle's son is my nephew.

My mother is my son's grandmother.

My brother is my nephew's father.

My sister's son is my son's cousin.

Version 2

Each student has either the beginning or the end of a sentence and must find the person with the rest of that sentence.

Time: 20 minutes
Level: Beginning and up
Main teaching points: Use family vocabulary
Understand possessives
Organization: Individuals, pairs, groups, whole class
Preparation: Prepare the strips in Box 21, cutting them between the beginning and the end of the sentence as indicated. If there are more than 18 students in the class, make extra copies so that each student will have one strip. Because it is often hard to predict how many students will attend a given class session, you may want to put the beginnings of sentences in one envelope and the ends in another.

Procedure

1. Have each student choose a strip.
2. Tell the students to stand up and walk around the room, telling others (not showing them) what is on their strip. When they find a person whose sentence completes theirs, they should sit down together. Ask each pair to read their sentences aloud to see that everyone has the correct match.

Follow-up: Have students create their own sentence strips.

Note: If you use a paper clip to keep the strips in order, you can simply count off the number of strips you will need just before doing the activity and mix them up in the envelopes.

BOX 21

Sentence strips

My mother's sister is	my aunt
My mother's brother is	my uncle
My sister's son is	my nephew
My sister's daughter is	my niece
My daughter's husband is	my son-in-law
My son's wife is	my daughter-in-law
My wife's mother is	my mother-in-law
My mother's mother is	my grandmother
My aunt's daughter is	my cousin

Copyright © Cambridge University Press.

Family tree

Each student represents his family with a family tree and then explains it to a partner.

Time: 30 to 45 minutes
Level: Beginning and up
Main teaching points: Learn family tree conventions
       Describe family relationships
       Use possessives
Organization: Individuals, pairs, whole class
Preparation: Find or make a family tree (many language textbooks provide them, or make one using your own family) as a model. You may want to supply students with unlined drawing paper.

Procedure

1. Show the students the model family tree. Work with them to discuss the relationships of the people in the family. They may ask each other questions about it, such as "Who is the grandfather's son?" If they have done the Family Strips activity, they could practice using the sentences modeled there.
2. Ask each student to draw a family tree for his family. This should include the names of the family members as well as their relationship to the student.
3. As students finish drawing, assign them to partners. Have each student explain his family tree to his partner. Tell the partner to ask questions to clarify the information or to find out more.
4. Assign new partners and have the students again tell about their families.
5. Bring the whole class together again and ask students to tell something they learned about their partners' families.

Stand-up family tree

Students arrange themselves into a family tree based on assigned roles.

Time: 20 minutes
Level: Beginning to intermediate
Main teaching points: Use family vocabulary
       Negotiate
       Use possessive adjectives
       Use possessive 's
Organization: Individuals, groups

Preparation: You will need a card for each student. On each card, write the name of a family member (grandmother, daughter, etc.). Be sure that you have sufficient space to do this activity. You may want to use a hallway or outdoor area. If you have a large class, provide roles for all of the students by having more than one family tree. The roles can be written on different colors of cards or with different colors of ink to denote different "families."

Procedure

1. Give each student a card identifying a family member.
2. Tell the students to arrange themselves as a family tree. Leave it to the students to negotiate placement. After everybody is in place, ask students to describe their relationships to others (Maria is my niece, etc.).

Photographs

Each student brings family pictures to talk about.

Time: 30 to 45 minutes
Level: Beginning and up
Main teaching points: Share family information
　　　　　　　　　　　Describe relationships and people
　　　　　　　　　　　Ask and answer questions
Organization: Pairs or threes, whole class
Preparation: Ask students to bring pictures of family members to class. It is a good idea to limit the number of pictures to four or five. If students bring more, they may choose the best ones to talk about. If they do not have any, they may draw some or simply describe one or two family members.

Procedure

1. Before dividing students into pairs or threes to look at the pictures, elicit from the class some questions or comments they might want to make about their classmates' photographs and write them on the board. A basic format for describing the pictures can be provided for lower-level students: "This is my son. His name is＿＿＿＿＿＿＿. He is＿＿＿ years old."
2. Divide the class into pairs or threes. Each student is to tell about his pictures. Encourage partners to comment and ask questions about the pictures.

≫→

3. Regroup students to repeat the activity. This can be done more than once.
4. When the students have had time to look at and comment on the pictures, bring the whole class together and ask students to tell what they have learned about their classmates in this activity.

Follow-up: Students write about a member of their own family or about a member of a partner's family.

Family numbers

Students dictate personally meaningful numbers to the class, and the other students try to guess the significance of the numbers.

Time: 15 to 20 minutes
Level: Beginning and up
Main teaching points: Share family information
                                    Ask questions
Organization: Individuals, small groups, whole class
Preparation: None

Procedure

1. Ask the students to write down at least two numbers, and up to five if they can, which relate to themselves or their families (for example, the number of siblings or children they have, their age, an important year).
2. Send one student to the board. Ask another student to dictate his numbers to the person at the board.
3. Ask the class to guess the meaning of the numbers for the student who gave them.
4. Continue with other students going to the board as their classmates dictate numbers.

Variation: In large classes the dictation and guessing may be done in small groups after the activity has been modeled by the teacher.

Family riddles

Students read and try to solve some family-related riddles.

Time: 20 minutes
Level: High beginning and up
Main teaching points: Read and solve problems
                        Discuss possible solutions
Organization: Individuals, whole class
Preparation: Choose one riddle from Box 22 and write it on a large
  piece of paper.

Procedure

1. Post the riddle before class.
2. As students arrive, point the riddle out to them. Encourage them to
   talk to each other about it.
3. When several people have solutions, discuss them together. If
   students wish to copy down the riddle, allow time for them to do
   so.

BOX 22*

Riddles

1. Mr. Jones tells everyone that he is the brother of a famous scientist. But Mr. Jones doesn't have a brother. Do you think he is lying?

2. Two fathers and two sons went fishing. Each of them caught one fish. The total number of fish they caught was three. How is this possible?

3. If the only sister of your mother's only brother has only one child, how is that person related to you?

4. A man is driving his son to school. There is a terrible accident. The father is killed instantly. His son is badly injured. They take the son to the emergency room at the hospital. They decide to operate on him. When they take him to the operating room, the doctor sees the boy and says, "I can't operate on him. He is my son." Who is the doctor?

*Riddle 4 can be used in English, where the word "doctor" does not indicate gender; it will not work in a language where that is not the case.

Answers: 1. Mr. Jones' sister is the famous scientist. 2. This is a grandfather, a father, and a son. The grandfather and father are both fathers and the father and son are both sons. 3. The child is you. 4. The doctor is the child's mother.

What is a family?

Students create a definition of a family individually and then contribute to a pair/group definition.

Time: 45 minutes
Level: Intermediate and up

Main teaching points: Explore the make-up of families
Write definitions
Discuss differences

Organization: Individuals, pairs, groups, whole class
Preparation: None

Procedure

1. Write on the board the following sentence starter.

   A family is _____ .

2. Ask the students to finish the sentence individually with a definition of family.
3. Divide the students into groups of three or four and ask them to compare their definitions.
4. Ask the groups to choose the definition they like best or to combine their definitions to create a new one.
5. Ask each group to read out the definition the members have agreed on and also to write them on the board or a large sheet of paper.
6. Write the situations in Box 23 on the board and ask each group to use their definition to decide whether each one is a family or not.
7. Ask the groups to report back their answers to the whole class. Allow time for groups to modify their definitions in the light of the discussion.

BOX 23

What is a family? – situations

1. A husband and wife without children
2. A father raising his children alone
3. Grandparents raising a child
4. A husband, wife, and two children living together
5 A mother and her adult child who live in different countries
6. A couple with children from previous marriages
7. A grandmother, an aunt and uncle, a husband and wife, their children, and the spouse and children of one of their children

Family member pie graphs

Students prepare pie graphs based on daily activities and then discuss them in pairs.

Time: 30 minutes
Level: Intermediate and up
Main teaching points: Classify and represent information
Describe habits
Use simple present tense
Organization: Individuals, pairs
Preparation: Prepare an example of a pie graph showing your own daily activities (see example in Box 24), plus two blank pie charts for each student. Rulers and colored pencils may also be helpful.

Procedure

1. Ask the students to look at and interpret the sample pie graph. Talk about how much of the person's day is spent on each type of activity.
2. Brainstorm a list of activities that the students do every day and write them on the board.
3. Ask the students to draw a pie graph for a typical day in their own lives and to discuss it with a partner.
4. Ask each student to draw a pie graph for a typical day in the life of a close family member and share both graphs with a new partner.
5. Assign new partners and repeat the comparison of both graphs.
6. Bring the whole class together and have the students discuss differences between their own lives and those of their family members.

Follow-up: Have students write sentences comparing their lives to those of other family members. Simple sentence frames can be provided for lower-level students, whereas more advanced students should be encouraged to write longer compositions.

BOX 24

Example of a pie chart based on daily activities

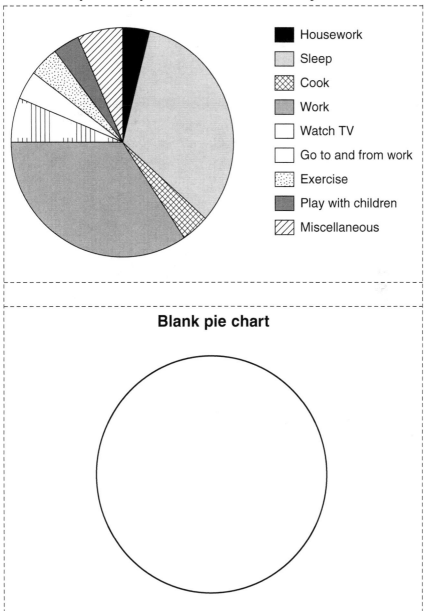

Housework
Sleep
Cook
Work
Watch TV
Go to and from work
Exercise
Play with children
Miscellaneous

Blank pie chart

A family problem

Groups of students engage in problem solving based on incremental written input.

Time: 45 minutes
Level: Intermediate and up
Main teaching points: Give and support opinions
                         Agree and disagree
                         Use modals
Organization: Groups, whole class
Preparation: Prepare a set of information cards (Box 25) for each group of three to five students. The number of the card should be written on the back of each card and they should be stacked in order, with number 1 at the top when the cards are upside down.

Procedure

1. Divide the class into groups of three to five students. Give each group a set of cards, placed face down on the table, with number 1 on top.
2. Explain that they are going to read about a family problem and discuss it step by step. They are to begin by looking at card number 1 and discussing it. When they have finished discussing that card, they can go on to number 2 and so on through the stack.
3. When all groups have completed the exercise, ask them to tell about their discussion. Did their opinions change? On what basis?

Follow-up: Students write a letter to the author suggesting their solutions to the problems. The letters can be written individually or in groups.

Notes

1. Some groups may move through the cards more quickly than others. If you see that this is happening, stop the group and ask them to discuss the problem more thoroughly, giving reasons for their opinions. Engage them in questions that force them to explore their opinions more carefully.
2. For a similar activity used with the theme of money, see page 221.

BOX 25

Information cards

1. "I have one brother, who is younger than I am. When I was 22, I got married and moved away from the town where my parents lived. My brother stayed in that town. My mother died when she was 80. My brother and his wife invited my father to live with them so they could take care of him."

   Do you think it was a good idea for the father to live with them? After you talk about it, look at card number 2.

2. "My brother asked my father to pay him $200 a month for rent and food."

   What do you think about that?

   Now look at card number 3.

3. "Sometimes my brother and his wife took my father out for dinner at expensive restaurants. They used his credit card to pay for it."

   What do you think about that?

   Now look at card number 4.

4. "They asked my father to sign a paper giving them the power to make financial decisions for him."

   Does this seem like a good idea?

   My father asked my opinion. What do you think I should tell him?

   Now look at card number 5.

5. "Last month my brother and his wife took a long and expensive vacation and left their children at home for my father to take care of."

   What do you think about the situation now?

   Look at card number 6.

➤

BOX 25 (continued)

6. "After they came back, my father asked to look at his financial records. He discovered that my brother had taken money from him."

What advice would you give the writer now?

What should she say to her brother?

What should she say to her father?

Go on to card number 7.

7. "I think he should call the police, but my father doesn't want to. He says it's not important since they're giving him a home and they're family."

What do you think is the best solution?

Community

It is essential that newcomers get to know the community in which they live. In their daily lives, they must go from place to place in order to work, to transact business, to shop, and to spend their leisure time. The second language class provides a setting in which they can learn about and explore their new home along with other newcomers and thus gain the knowledge and skills they need. There are innumerable sources of information about your community, many of which can be easily adapted for class use. This unit includes activities designed specifically to use materials from your own community.

Fuzzy photos

Students try to identify community landmarks from out-of-focus pictures.

Time: 15 to 20 minutes
Level: Beginning and up
Main teaching points: Identify community landmarks
Use yes/no questions
Organization: Whole class
Preparation: Prepare a number of slides or overhead transparencies of local landmarks. (See "Variations" for less high-tech alternatives.)

Procedure

1. Adjust the projector so that it is deliberately out of focus and then put one of the pictures on the projector.
2. Ask the students to guess what is in the picture. Encourage them to use question forms using the verb "to be" – for example, "Is it the _____?
3. When they begin to run out of suggestions, bring the picture slightly more into focus and encourage them to guess again.
4. Gradually bring the picture into focus until someone guesses correctly.
5. Put the picture fully into focus and then ask the students what they

know about this landmark. Make notes on the board of the information they give.

6. Repeat the procedure with another picture.

Variations: In the absence of overhead or slide projectors, use one of the following variations.

1. Pictures can be cut up and students can try to guess the overall picture from the parts, which are revealed one piece at a time.
2. The teacher can hold the picture facing toward her, and then "flash" it for a split second to the class. This may be repeated several times for longer or shorter time intervals.

Follow-up: Ask the students to write about one or more of the landmarks. Beginning students may make use of the notes on the board to help them.

Photo questions

Students generate questions related to the content of community photographs

Time: 20 to 30 minutes
Level: Beginning and up
Main teaching points: Learn about the local community
                             Ask questions
Organization: Pairs
Preparation: Prepare a number of pictures showing the local community. You may use the same photos as in Fuzzy Photos (page 73) or Community Photos (page 88) supplemented with pictures of people and places in the community. Each picture should be mounted on a piece of paper so that there is a band of paper showing around the photograph. Each pair of students will need at least one picture. You also need one large picture or poster that all the students can see.

Procedure

1. Post the large picture in the middle of the blackboard and ask the students to ask "Wh" questions about the picture and its contents – for example, "Where was this taken?" "What time of day was it?" "Who are the people?" "Why are they_____?" As the students ask the questions, write them around the perimeter of the picture.
2. Divide the students into pairs and give one of the pictures to each pair.
3. Ask the pairs to brainstorm as many questions as they can and to

write them around the perimeter of the picture. Encourage them not to limit themselves to easily answerable questions.

4. Have the pairs share their pictures and questions in groups and speculate on the answers.
5. Post the pictures and questions on the wall and have the students circulate and read each others' questions.
6. Give the students any information you have about the pictures.

Follow-ups

1. Pairs may exchange pictures and try to answer each others' questions.
2. Students may provide their own pictures and invite other students to write questions about them. These pictures may be of communities in their native countries or in their new country.

Do-it-yourself matching

Students use material from their own community to match pictures and text.

Time: 15 to 20 minutes
Level: Beginning and up (depending on the difficulty of the text selected)
Main teaching points: Learn about the community
                Sequence stages in a process
                Use imperatives
Organization: Individuals, pairs
Preparation: Find directions from your community that include pictures and written text. For example, the telephone book might include calling instructions, local transportation companies may publish brochures about using buses or subways (see example in Box 26), banks may provide ATM instructions, a city may provide recycling information, the motor vehicle department might have posters showing road signs). Make a copy of the page. Separate the pictures from the text and glue the text to a piece of paper. Cut out the pictures and tape or glue them to the same piece of paper, but not in the same order as the text. Make copies of this revised sheet, one for each student or pair of students.

Procedure

1. Give each student or pair of students a copy of the sheet. Instruct them to draw a line between the text and the matching picture.
2. Have the students compare their answers with those of neighboring students.

⋙➔

BOX 26

Bus fare card example

New Electronic Fareboxes

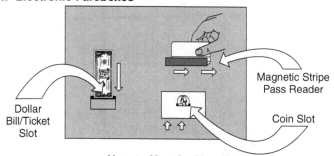

Magnetic Stripe
Pass Reader

Dollar
Bill/Ticket
Slot

Coin Slot

How to Use the New Farebox

When paying with a magnetically encoded pass, make sure the stripe is facing you when it is passed through the card reader. This feature relieves the driver from visually inspecting your pass each time you board.

Listen for the "beep" sound after you pay your fare. The farebox will sound a "beep" which tells you and the driver that the correct fare has been paid.

Insert only coins into the coin slot. Never insert paper or tickets into the coin slot.

Have your fare ready to insert into the farebox when you board the bus.

Please insert all cash fares into the box. Drivers are not permitted to accept your fares. Have the exact amount ready. Neither the driver nor the farebox can make change.

If you are paying with a dollar bill, open it full length and insert it into the bill slot – either side up.

Hopes and fears

Students make predictions for the various communities to which they belong.

Time: 30 to 40 minutes
Level: Beginning and up
Main teaching points: Examine community membership
　　　　　　　　　　　Use future tenses
　　　　　　　　　　　Construct sentences with "hope" and "fear"
Organization: Individuals, pairs, whole class
Preparation: None

Procedure

1. Draw the chart in Box 27 on the board and ask the students to copy it, leaving plenty of room to write in each box.
2. Have the students brainstorm the different communities to which they belong – for example *family, workplace, neighborhood, city, country, world.*
3. Ask each student to select four of the communities on the board and to write one in each of the boxes numbered 1 to 4 on their chart.
4. Instruct the students to write in each box the good things they expect to happen in that community in the time frame indicated.
5. When they have completed this task, ask the students to draw a second grid and to write in the bad things they expect to happen in each community.
6. Have them explain and compare their grids in pairs.

Variation: Lower level students may be asked to complete only the "hopes" section of the exercise.
Follow-up: Students can write about their hopes and fears for the future.

BOX 27

Hopes and fears grid

	Today	Next week	Next year	My lifetime	My children's lifetime
1.					
2.					
3.					
4.					

Community map

In this activity, students draw and compare their views of their new home.

Time: 30 to 40 minutes
Level: High beginning and up
Main teaching points: Get acquainted with the community
Make comparisons
Organization: Individuals, pairs, groups, whole class
Preparation: None

Procedure

1. Ask the students, working individually, to draw a map of the city in which they live (or, in a large city, a familiar portion of it). As they draw, walk around the class. Reassure them that their maps may be

different from those of other students and that the maps should reflect their own ideas.

2. Divide the class into pairs and have each student explain his map to his partner.
3. Assign new partners and ask the students to explain their maps again.
4. Bring the whole class together and ask them to describe differences between their maps and their partners'.
5. Ask the students to work collaboratively to draw a map of the city. If the class is small, have the whole class work together at the board; if it is large, divide them into groups of five or six to work on large pieces of paper.

Follow-up: Have the students compare their maps with actual maps of the city, locating streets or landmarks on both of them.

Favorite places

In this survey, students interview each other and people outside the class to find out what their favorite places in the community are.

Time: 15 to 20 minutes in class, 15 minutes outside of class
Level: High beginning and up
Main teaching points: Share information about the community
 Ask and answer questions
Organization: Pairs
Preparation: Prepare two copies of Box 28 for each student, or write the material on the board or on a large sheet of paper for the students to copy.

Procedure

1. Hand out one copy of the grid to each student or post it for students to copy. Explain that this will be the basis for an interview of a classmate.
2. Divide the students into pairs.
3. Have each student interview his partner about a favorite place and record the information on the grid.
4. Have each student interview someone outside the class and report back their findings.

Follow-up: Students may write their own surveys to find out such things as where people work, shop, recreate, and eat; what different groups of people are in the community; where different groups of people live; where children play; where teenagers meet or spend time; and where older people get together.

≫→

BOX 28

Favorite places: interview questions

Questions	Answers
1. What is your favorite place in this city?	
2. Where is it?	
3. Why do you like to go there?	
4. What do you do there?	
5. Who goes there?	
6. When do you like to go there?	
7. How much does it cost?	
8. What other information would you like to give about this place?	

Do-it-yourself information gap

Students complete an information gap activity based on local information.

Time: 20 minutes
Level: High beginning and up
Main teaching points: Share information about the community
                       Ask and answer questions
Organization: Pairs
Preparation: Choose a grid containing information about your community (such as a TV guide, information about a place to visit, a schedule for a clinic, times and ticket prices for an event). Make a photocopy of it. Designate one of the copies "A" and the other "B." On the A form, white-out some of the information; on the B form, white-out other information. Form A should contain the information that has been deleted from B and vice versa. Make enough copies of A for half the students and of B for the remainder. (See Box 29 for an example.)

Procedure

1. Divide the class into pairs. Give one person of each pair the A form and the other the B form. Tell them not to show each other their papers.
2. Explain that the students are to ask questions that will give them information to put in the blank spaces on their papers.
3. After a pair has finished filling in the blanks, they may compare their papers and correct them.

Variation: In a lower-level class, limit the blanks to familiar material such as numbers and rehearse the questions the students will need to ask.

BOX 29

Information gap model

Person A

Channel	7:00	7:30	8:00	8:30	9:00
4		North Carolina Now			
5	An Equal Education for All?			Coach	Top Cops
6	Wheel of Fortune		The Cosby Show		Dateline
13	Beverly Hills		Matlock	The Lady Killer	
27	Rockford Files			The 20th Century	

Person B

Channel	7:00	7:30	8:00	8:30	9:00
4	Business Report			Mystery	
5			Star Trek		Top Cops
6		Jeopardy		Mysteries	Dateline
13		90210	Matlock		
27	Rockford Files	Biography			

BOX 29 (continued)

KEY

Channel	7:00	7:30	8:00	8:30	9:00
4	Business Report	North Carolina Now		Mystery	
5	An Equal Education for All?		Star Trek	Coach	Top Cops
6	Wheel of Fortune	Jeopardy	The Cosby Show	Mysteries	Dateline
13	Beverly Hills	90210	Matlock	The Lady Killer	
27	Rockford Files	Biography		The 20th Century	

What do you look for in a neighborhood?

Students discuss what makes a good community.

Time: 20 to 30 minutes.
Level: High beginning and up
Main teaching points: Share opinions
Use comparisons
Categorize
Organization: Individuals, groups, whole class
Preparation: None

Procedure

1. Draw the categorization grid (Box 30) on the board and have the students copy it.
2. Dictate the list of factors (Box 31) to the students and invite them to add any other factors they can think of.
3. Have the students, working individually, put each factor in the appropriate box according to whether it is in their opinion *essential, nice but not necessary,* or *unwanted.*
4. Have the students compare their selections in groups.
5. Have the groups report back to the whole class.

Follow-up: Have the students rank their choices in the *essential* column and discuss them in groups.

》》➔

BOX 30

Categorization grid

Essential	Nice but not necessary	Unwanted

BOX 31

Neighborhood factors

Places of worship	Jobs	People who speak your language	Safety
Family	Low-cost housing	Recreation facilities	Schools
Friends	Night life	Restaurants	Shopping
Health care	Parks		Public transportation

Places and labels*

Students place adjectives on a map of the city or area in which they live.

Time: 30 to 40 minutes
Level: Intermediate
Main teaching points: Share ideas about the community
                              Express agreement and disagreement
                              Use adjectives
                              Use comparatives
Organization: Individuals, groups, whole class
Preparation: You will need a large map of the city or area and, for each student, six Post-it notes or six small pieces of paper (plus pins, tacks, or tape to attach them to the map), plus a vocabulary list for each student (see Box 32).

Procedure

1. Post the map on the classroom wall.
2. Give each student a copy of the vocabulary list and six Post-it notes or small pieces of paper.
3. Ask each student to pick six words from the list and write one on each paper. The student should then place the words on the map.
4. Divide the students into groups of three or four and have them discuss the adjectives they chose and why they placed them where they did.
5. Have the groups report back to the whole class. Encourage the students to discuss differences of opinion, as well as feelings aroused by different parts of the city or area and the source of these feelings. Explore the overall patterns that emerge.

Variations

1. The vocabulary list can be modified to accommodate higher- or lower-level learners.
2. In a large class, use more than one map and/or fewer slips of paper per student.

Follow-up: The same activity may be used with other maps: neighborhood maps, country maps, regional maps, world maps.

                                                      ⠀⟫➔

---

*This activity is based on an idea in *Priorities for Development*, Development Education Center, Selly Oak, Birmingham, U.K., 1981.

BOX 32

Places and labels vocabulary

dangerous	pleasant	industrial	safe
beautiful	ugly	peaceful	noisy
inner city	poor	wealthy	depressed
exciting	residential	industrial	suburban
quiet	relaxed	scary	friendly
unfriendly	crowded	boring	lively
bad	good	popular	unpopular
affordable	expensive	accessible	inaccessible

Guide

Students work together to make a guide to the town they live in. The guide can be distributed to new students and to other students in the language program. This is a long-term project that will continue over several lessons.

Time: 30 to 60 minutes on each of four days
Level: Intermediate and up
Main teaching points: Collect and summarize information about the community
Write and edit a report
Organization: Individuals, groups, whole class
Preparation: Bring brochures, telephone books, newspapers, and other local resources. This project could be combined with a visit to the local public library to look for information.

Procedure

Day 1

1. Tell the students that they are going to make a guide to their city. It can be a general guide or it may be limited to a particular area of study (such as shopping or transportation).
2. Brainstorm what might be included. List the students' ideas on the board. With the class, decide how the work can be divided. In the

case of transportation, for example, buses, trains, subways, and cars might each constitute a different topic. Once the topics have been determined, discuss with the students where they can get information on the topic (the library, government or other offices, brochures, schedules, newspapers, interviews) and what kind of information they want to look for.

3. Have the students choose topics in which they are interested and group them accordingly. Students may have to work on their second-choice topics in order to make the numbers in each group more or less even. At the groups' first meeting, have them talk about their topic, the information they need, and where they can get it. Each group should make a plan for how they will proceed. Provide suggestions or resources as needed.

Day 2 (allow several days or a week between days 1 and 2, with reminders during the intervening classes)

1. Have the groups meet together and share their information. At this stage, they should also work on the organization of their topic: which chunks of information should go together and in what sequence.
2. Ask the groups to begin writing their section of the guide book. This can be done on paper, which can be copied and distributed to other groups, or on large sheets of paper or plastic, which can be posted on the walls.

Day 3 (the class following day 2)

1. Post or distribute copies of the drafts from the preceding day. Ask the class to put a question mark next to any part of the draft they don't understand, but not to change anything.
2. Divide the class into groups, with one member from each topic in each group. Have them go over the writing of each group, noting their queries. The member of the group whose writing is being discussed should make notes on his group's comments.
3. Send the students back to their topic groups to discuss the comments and revise their writing into its final form.

Day 4 (the class following day 3)

Copy and distribute the guide to the class.

Variation: For a high beginning class the topic should be limited to one that is being studied in class, and more support should be given in terms of resources.

Community photos

Students select photographs to illustrate their community.

Time: 30 to 40 minutes
Level: Intermediate and up
Main teaching points: Examine ways to represent the community
Use comparatives
Negotiate
Persuade
Organization: Individuals, pairs, groups, whole class
Preparation: Prepare a set of ten numbered photographs showing different aspects of the local area. These may be pictures you have taken yourself, or ones you have obtained from newspapers or magazines. Alternatively, you may use slides or overhead transparencies. Draw a copy of the chart in Box 33 on the board.

Procedure

1. Post the pictures on the wall or lay them out on a table so that the students can circulate and see them.
2. Ask the students, working individually, to select the three they think are most representative of the area and one that they think is not representative.
3. As the students finish making their selections, pair them up and ask them to compare their choices and to negotiate until they reach an agreement on three pictures they could use to represent the area and one they think is not representative.
4. As the pairs finish, combine them into groups of four and ask them to repeat the process.
5. Have the groups report back to the whole class the pictures they have selected and indicate their choices on the grid using check marks.
6. Have the whole class discuss areas of agreement/disagreement.

BOX 33

Community photos grid				
PICTURES	Group A	Group B	Group C	Group D
1.				
2.				
3.				
4.				
5.				
6.				
7.				
8.				
9.				
10.				

Food

Food is a topic that everyone loves and knows something about. In this unit, students practice naming foods and stating preferences, shopping for food, describing ways foods are cooked, and requesting foods they want. As they study about food, they also learn about expressions of quantity and about count and noncount nouns. Free materials, which can be used for teaching and for homework, are easily available in supermarkets and newspapers and in the kitchen cupboard. Students have an opportunity to share their cultures with their classmates as they compare customs regarding food.

Refrigerator dictation

Students draw the contents of a refrigerator.

Time: 10 to 15 minutes
Level: Beginning to intermediate
Main teaching points: Practice food vocabulary
                        Follow directions
Organization: Whole class
Preparation: None

Procedure

1. Be sure that the students know the following direction words: top, bottom, middle, below, left, right. Ask the students to name some items in their refrigerators.
2. Ask the students to take out paper and pencil. Draw a large refrigerator on the board with a freezer compartment at the top and three shelves inside. In a lower-level class, practice directions, such as "Which is the top shelf?"
3. Read the directions in Box 34 aloud, repeating as needed. After everybody has finished drawing, tell them to compare their drawings with a neighbor.
4. Ask individual students to go to the board and draw an item from the dictation as directed by a classmate who will tell the item and its location.

Variations

1. The teacher may describe what is in her own refrigerator.
2. Lower-level students can label the items in the refrigerator while higher-level students can write a spatial description of the contents of the refrigerator.

Follow-up: For further practice, this can be done as a pair dictation, with each member of the pair dictating items from his refrigerator to his partner.

BOX 34

Refrigerator dictation

1. Draw a large refrigerator. Put a freezer section at the top. Put three shelves inside it.
2. Draw three apples on the bottom shelf on the right.
3. Put a bottle of milk on the top shelf on the left.
4. Put a box of ice cream in the freezer.
5. Put a head of lettuce in the middle of the middle shelf.
6. Put a jar of jam on the top shelf in the middle.
7. Put five eggs to the right of the jam.
8. To the left of the lettuce, put two pieces of chicken.
9. Below the chicken, put a fish.

Who, what, and when

Students dictate information to each other on food and mealtimes.

Time: 10 minutes
Level: Beginning to intermediate
Main teaching points: Ask and answer questions
Share cultural information related to meals (in the follow-up)
Organization: Pairs
Preparation: Make one copy of Box 35 for every two students. Then cut the copies in half. Meal times and foods can be changed to suit the location of the class.

Procedure

1. Distribute the A sheets to half of the students and the B sheets to the other half. Point out that each form has different information, and their task is to ask and record the missing information from their partner.
2. Divide the students into pairs, an A with a B. Caution them not to show their papers to their partners, as this is a listening activity. Now instruct the students to ask their partners questions in order to complete the information on the chart.
3. Have them check their answers by comparing their papers.

Variations

1. For lower-level students, rehearse and write on the board the questions they will need to ask (When does Mary have lunch? What does Mary have for lunch?) after handing out the sheets and before beginning the dictation.
2. For higher-level students, white-out additional information, being sure that each item remains on one of the forms.

Follow-up: Ask students to write down the usual meal times in their countries as well as the names of foods that people typically eat for those meals. They can then share this information in small groups or with the entire class.

BOX 35

Information gap sheet

Form A

Name	Meal	Time	Food
Mary	Lunch		Soup and salad
John	Dinner	6:45	
Susan	Breakfast	7:25	
Lisa	Dinner		Steak and potatoes
Larry	Lunch	12:35	

Form B

Name	Meal	Time	Food
Mary	Lunch	12:15	
John	Dinner		Fried chicken
Susan	Breakfast		Cereal and milk
Lisa	Dinner	6:20	
Larry	Lunch		Hamburger

Shopping

Students draw and describe typical food markets in their countries.

Time: 30 to 40 minutes
Level: Beginning and up
Main teaching points: Share cultural information about food markets
                             Describe places
                             Use present tense
Organization: Individuals, pairs, whole class
Preparation: None

Procedure

1. Begin by asking students about shopping for food: How often do they shop for food here and in their country? Do they buy everything in one place or in different places here and in their country? Do they shop near their home or far from it?
2. Ask the students to draw a picture of the place at which they usually buy food in their country. As they are drawing, put the following questions on the board: Is the place you shop one big store or a lot of small shops? Do you pay for everything at one place? How are the departments or shops divided up? Can you buy everything (food, medicine, clothing, paper products, etc.) at one place?
3. As students finish drawing, assign each one to a partner. Tell them to describe their pictures and compare them with their partners'. They may use the questions on the board to help them.
4. For additional practice using these pictures, assign each student to a second partner and repeat the discussion.
5. Ask the whole class to share what they have learned about their classmates' countries.

Follow-up: After the activity is completed, ask more advanced students to write a description of the place where they shop. Beginning students can label their drawings or write a few sentences about them.

Supermarkets

Students listen to the description of a supermarket and label the location of each department on the plan.

Time: 20 minutes
Level: High beginning to intermediate
Main teaching points: Learn how supermarkets are arranged
                        Follow directions
Organization: Pairs or threes, whole class
Preparation: Make a copy of the store floor plan in Box 36 for each group. Write the department list on the board, omitting the numbers. Make a copy of the store cards for each group (Box 37 on page 97). Arrange them upside down with card 1 on top.

Procedure

1. Divide the class into pairs or threes. Hand out the store plan. Go over the list of departments to be sure the students understand all of them.
2. Hand out the store cards. Explain that the students are to pick up one card at a time and label the departments according to what they have read. One group member can read the card aloud, or the whole group can read it.
3. After the groups have completed the task, ask individual students to come to the board and write in the name of a department or to describe the location of a department to a classmate at the board.
4. Read the following list of items aloud and ask students where they would find them: cheese, rice, bananas, milk, sugar, ground beef, turkey, lettuce, cat food, noodles, shrimp, paper napkins, apples, tomatoes. Note that some of these may be found in more than one department.

»»→

BOX 36

Floor plan

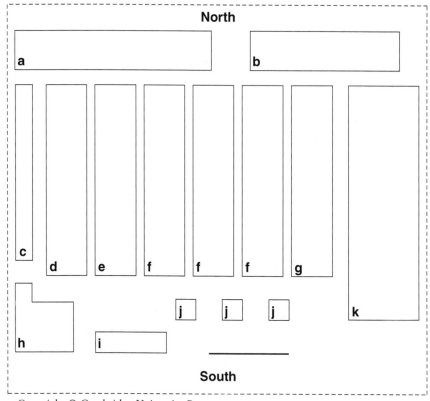

Key:

a. Meat, fish, and seafood

b. Deli (delicatessen)

c. Dairy

d. Frozen foods

e. Nonfood items

f. Canned and packaged foods

g. Imported and special foods

h. Baked goods

i. Customer service

j. Checkout

k. Produce

BOX 37

Cards

1. Enter the door, which is on the south side of the building and turn right. Along the east wall you will find the produce department. Write "produce."	6. After you pass packaged and canned foods on your left you will come to the nonfood area.
2. Turn left and walk north. On your left is the imported and special foods section.	7. Turn left at the west wall. On your left are frozen foods. Dairy products are on your right.
3. Straight ahead is the deli department.	8. In the southwest corner you will find baked goods. Turn left.
4. Turn left at the deli department. On your left you will see a large section of canned and packaged foods.	9. On your right after baked goods, you will find the customer service counter.
5. On your right you will see meat, fish, and seafood.	10. Finally, in the center on your right you will find the checkout area.

Food search

Students scan supermarket fliers. Fliers are multipage advertising brochures that supermarkets in the United States and some other countries distribute weekly. If supermarket fliers are not available, any kind of supermarket advertisement with specific items, quantities, and prices can be used.

Time: 15 to 20 minutes
Level: Beginning and up
Main teaching points: Learn food vocabulary
                        Learn units of measure
                        Scan for specific information
                        Classify
Organization: Individuals, pairs, or small groups
Preparation: Bring enough copies of supermarket fliers for each pair of students (or one for each person if possible). Ask your students to bring some too.

Procedure

1. Discuss scanning with the students. Ask them how they look for words in the dictionary or names in the telephone book. Do they read every word on the page? Tell them that in this activity they will be scanning for information.
2. Make a list on the board of the items the students are to scan for: one fruit, one vegetable, one meat, one dairy product, one snack food, and one nonfood item.
3. Distribute the fliers.
4. Tell the students to look as quickly as possible for the above and to note the item, the price, and the unit of measure (pound, pint, etc.).
5. Compare the items, prices, and units of measure that the students located.

Variations

1. For lower-level students, list specific foods (apples, chicken) and reduce the number of items they are to locate.
2. Tell higher-level students to find twenty different foods and list them by category (fruit, vegetable, etc.), along with the price and unit of measure.

Shopping list

Students use supermarket fliers to "shop" for food. *If supermarket fliers are not available, any kind of supermarket advertisement with specific items, quantities, and prices can be used.*

Time: 20 to 30 minutes
Level: High beginning
Main teaching points: Learn consumer skills
                                  Learn weights and measures
                                    Scan for specific information
                                    Write down dictation
Organization: Small groups
Preparation: Have a supermarket flier available for each group. If possible, have fliers from different stores. Make up a shopping list for the class based on what is advertised in the flier, using local weights and measures (see the sample list in Box 38).

Procedure

1. Dictate the shopping list to the students.
2. Divide the class into groups of three or four. Give each group a supermarket flier. The task for each group is to find each of the foods and write down its cost, then calculate the total.
3. Bring the whole class together to compare results.

Variation: For lower-level students, post the list on a large sheet of paper. The list can be shortened or modified.

                                                       »→

BOX 38

Sample shopping list

1 bunch of broccoli

About 1 pound of fresh or canned green beans

2 liters of a soft drink

2 pounds of sweet potatoes

A 10-pound turkey or a 5-pound leg of lamb

1 dozen eggs

1 jar of peanut butter

1 jar of jam

1½ pounds of steak

2 packages of frozen peas

5 pounds of apples

1 6-ounce can of tuna fish

Food bingo

Students look for food words using a bingo format.

Time: 30 to 40 minutes
Level: Intermediate
Main teaching points: Understand definitions
                        Follow directions
Organization: Whole class
Preparation: None

Procedure

1. Read each description in Box 39 to the class and ask the students to identify the food it describes.
2. On the board, draw a bingo grid with twenty-five boxes, five horizontal and five vertical, as on a bingo card. Instruct the students to copy the grid, making each box large enough to write in a word.
3. Dictate the words on the list in Box 40 on page 104, telling the students to write one word in each box in any order. Model this with the grid on the board. There will be one "free" box, in the middle.
4. Explain to the students that you are going to read a description of each word. As you read the description, the students will mark a small X in the corner of the box with the matching word. The object of the game is to get five squares in a row, vertically, horizontally, or diagonally. When students get five in a row, they should call out "Food!"
5. Begin the game by reading the descriptions in any order, marking them off as you do so. When a student announces that he has won, have him read back the words he has marked. The game can be repeated once or twice, with the students marking the squares in different ways, as with an O or a horizontal line.

Variation: For lower-level students, write the words on the board for the students to copy. Read the words themselves rather than their descriptions.

⟫→

BOX 39

Descriptions

1. This is a small, red, sweet fruit that grows close to the ground. It is often used in ice cream, pie, or shortcake.
2. This is a long, orange, crunchy vegetable that grows under the ground. People eat it raw or cooked.
3. This vegetable is usually brown on the outside and white on the inside. It has a round shape. It grows under the ground. People eat it many different ways: baked, fried, mashed, or as chips.
4. This meat comes from a bird. You can fry it or roast it or broil it. It also makes good soup.
5. People like to eat these green leaves in salad. It is usually eaten raw.
6. This round fruit grows on a tree. It is orange. People eat it raw or make juice from it.
7. This comes from a bird. It is round and white on the outside and orange inside. People eat it many ways, such as fried, scrambled, soft boiled, or hard boiled.
8. This is a long, yellow fruit. The inside is white and soft. People eat the inside but not the outside. It is usually eaten raw.
9. When this animal is alive, it can swim. It does not have any legs. Some people like to catch it.
10. This is really a fruit, but we think of it as a vegetable. It is red and round. We eat it raw in salads. We sometimes cook a sauce with it to put on spaghetti. We mix it with many other foods.
11. This is a frozen dessert made with milk or cream. Chocolate, strawberry, and vanilla are popular flavors.
12. You can use this food to make toast or a sandwich. If you make a sandwich, you put meat or cheese or other ingredients between two pieces of this.
13. This is a kind of long noodle or pasta. It is often prepared with a tomato sauce.

BOX 39 (continued)

14. This is a hot liquid made from meat or vegetables. You can eat it with a spoon or drink it from a cup.
15. This is a kind of meat, usually beef. You can eat it rare or medium or well done.
16. This is a hot brown liquid. Some people like it with milk or sugar. It contains caffeine. Many people drink it in the morning to help them wake up.
17. This is a very important food in many countries. It is in the form of small white pieces. You can steam it or boil it. People eat it alone or with vegetables or meat.
18. This is an Italian food. The bottom part is like bread. On top of that are tomato and cheese and sometimes other vegetables or meat.
19. This is a white liquid. You can drink it hot or cold. It comes from a cow.
20. This is a round crunchy fruit that grows on a tree. It can be yellow, green, or red. People eat it raw or cook it. Sometimes they use it to make pie.
21. These are small and juicy. You buy them in bunches. People usually eat them raw. You can make juice or wine with them. They may be found in many colors: yellow, red, purple, or green.
22. This is a kind of hot sandwich with ground beef and perhaps onions and lettuce and tomato. It is popular in fast-food restaurants.
23. This is a yellow fruit that is not sweet. People use the juice for cooking. They also put it in their tea or on fish. Some people like it in pie.
24. This is a popular vegetable in the United States. The Indians first grew it. It is usually yellow or white, but sometimes it is blue or red. You buy it by the ear.

BOX 40

Foods

strawberry	carrot	potato	chicken
lettuce	orange	eggs	banana
fish	tomato	ice cream	bread
spaghetti	soup	steak	coffee
rice	pizza	milk	apple
grape	hamburger	lemon	corn

Copyright © Cambridge University Press.

Food proverbs

Students read and interpret food proverbs.

Time: 5 to 10 minutes each
Level: Intermediate and up
Main teaching points: Learn proverbs
                       Explain and restate
Organization: Individuals, small groups, whole class
Preparation: Select one proverb from Box 41 and copy it onto a large strip of paper.

Procedure

1. Post the proverb on the wall as students are coming into class.
2. Give them a few minutes to think about and to talk over with classmates what the proverb means and when it might be used. In many cases students may have the same proverb or a slightly different one in their own language (e.g., "An onion a day keeps the doctor away").
3. Have the class as a whole compare their conclusions.

Variation: Ask higher-level students to paraphrase the proverb. Have them compare their paraphrases in small groups and choose the best one to put on the board.

Follow-ups

1. In a higher-level class, have the students read all of the proverbs and then choose one they think is particularly meaningful. Have them write about it, first explaining what it means and then giving examples of when it might be used.
2. Ask students to bring other food proverbs from their native cultures and translate them into English for discussion.

BOX 41

Food proverbs

An apple a day keeps the doctor away.
Don't bite the hand that feeds you.
Don't cry over spilled milk.
Don't put all your eggs in one basket.
Half a loaf is better than none.
One man's meat is another man's poison.
Too many cooks spoil the soup.
Variety is the spice of life.
You can lead a horse to water but you can't make him drink.
Don't count your chickens until they are hatched.
You can't make an omelet without breaking eggs.
You can't have your cake and eat it.
Enough is as good as a feast.
Man cannot live by bread alone.

Recipe dictation

Students listen to and write down a recipe.

Time: 20 to 30 minutes
Level: High beginning and up
Main teaching points: Learn recipe format
Follow directions
Organization: Whole class
Preparation: Choose a recipe you think your students would like (see Box 42 for an example). Write the ingredients on a large sheet of paper or on the board, omitting the numbers and measurements and words that are familiar to the students but leaving space for them to be written in later. If you like, bring a pan and the measuring utensils that are needed, as well as any ingredients that may be unfamiliar to the students. You may also want to prepare the food and bring it to class for the students to sample.

Procedure

1. Post the recipe.
2. Have the students copy the recipe from the model, leaving blanks to be filled in later.
3. Read the recipe aloud and have the students fill in the blanks on their paper. Repeat parts of the recipe as needed.
4. When you have finished reading, have the students take turns completing the dictation on the board and correcting their papers.

Variations

1. Give beginning students a sheet with the ingredients and the measures (cups, etc.) with only numbers omitted.
2. Advanced students can write down the entire recipe from dictation.

BOX 42

Recipe: Easy Chocolate Cake

You will need a cake pan that is <u>9</u> inches (21 centimeters) square. You will also need a measuring cup, a teaspoon, and a tablespoon. Before you start, set the oven to <u>350°F</u> (180°C).

Ingredients:

<u>1½</u> cups (210 grams) flour

<u>3</u> tablespoons cocoa

<u>1</u> teaspoon baking soda

<u>1</u> cup (200 grams) sugar

<u>½</u> teaspoon salt

<u>5</u> tablespoons (78 milliliters) cooking oil

<u>1</u> tablespoon vinegar

<u>1</u> teaspoon vanilla

<u>1</u> cup (250 milliliters) cold water

1. Put the dry ingredients (flour, cocoa, baking soda, sugar, and salt) in the baking pan and mix them together.
2. Pour the liquids (oil, vinegar, vanilla, and water) over the top.
3. Mix everything together until all the dry ingredients are wet and are the same color. Be sure to check the corners of the pan.
4. Put the cake in the oven and bake for 30 minutes. You can tell if it is done by poking the middle of the cake with a toothpick. If the toothpick comes out clean, the cake is done.
5. Let the cake cool.

Cookbook

Students prepare a cookbook of favorite recipes from their countries.

Time: 30 to 40 minutes on each of three or four days
Level: Beginning and up
Main teaching points: Write directions
　　　　　　　　　　　Use imperatives
　　　　　　　　　　　Edit
Organization: Small groups, whole class
Preparation: Prepare posters with cooking instruction words such as stir, beat, mix, add, bake, preheat, chop, mince, and so on. Additional words may be elicited from the students. The recipe from the recipe dictation (Box 42 on page 107) can be used as a model.

Procedure

1. Be sure that all the students understand the conventions for writing recipes, as well as the meanings of the instruction words.
2. Students may work alone or with classmates from the same country.
3. Tell the students to choose a favorite recipe (preferably not too complex) and write it down in English.
4. After students finish writing the recipes, have them exchange them with other groups or individuals. Tell the readers to read the recipes carefully to see if they are clear and easily followed. The readers may note suggestions for the writers. If class members like to cook, they can try out the recipes to see if the instructions are clear.
5. After this initial editing, copy the recipes so that the whole class can look at all of them to be sure that they are clear and that they follow the same format.
6. When all editing is finished, print the final product to share with the class and with others.

Restaurant questionnaire

Students interview each other about eating in restaurants.

Time: 10 to 15 minutes
Level: High beginning to intermediate
Main teaching points: Share personal information
　　　　　　　　　　　Ask and answer questions
Organization: Pairs, whole class
Preparation: Make copies of the questionnaire in Box 43 for all of the students.

Procedure

1. Divide students into pairs.
2. Distribute the questionnaires. Tell the students to ask their partners the questions on the questionnaire and to note down their answers.
3. After they have finished, bring the whole class together to tell what they learned from their partners.

Variation: To make the activity more challenging, dictate the questions rather than copying them.

BOX 43

Restaurant questionnaire

Ask your partner the following questions:

1. Do you prefer to eat at home or in a restaurant? Why?

2. Does the rest of your family prefer to eat at home or in a restaurant? Why?

3. What kind of restaurant do you like to go to?

4. What kind of restaurant do others in your family like to go to?

5. How often do you eat in a restaurant in this country? In your country?

6. When do you go to restaurants?

7. What do you like to order in a restaurant?

Yellow Pages

Students use the Yellow Pages of the telephone book to learn about restaurants.

Time: 20 to 40 minutes
Level: High beginning and up
Main teaching points: Use a telephone book
　　　　　　　　　　　Classify information
　　　　　　　　　　　Ask and answer questions
Organization: Individuals or pairs, whole group
Preparation: Cut or copy enough advertisements for restaurants from the Yellow Pages of your local telephone book for pairs of students to share or, in a small class, for each student. If possible, bring one or more intact copies of the Yellow Pages to class and multiple copies of a city map.

Procedure

1. Show the students the Yellow Pages and ask them what kind of information they contain and how they are organized. If you have multiple copies, have students find the restaurant section and tell what they find there.
2. Draw the grid in Box 44 on the board, with a row for each restaurant.
3. Hand out the advertisements. Ask the students to read their advertisements and find the information indicated on the grid. "Special information" may include such things as whether credit cards are accepted, the hours the restaurant is open, or the kind of food it serves.
4. When they have located the information, each student or pair can fill it in on the grid. The grid can then serve as a basis for practicing questions and answers (either teacher or student generated), such as "Where is the City Cafe?" If a city map is available, students can locate the restaurants on the map.

Variation: The same activity can be done with labels from bottles, cans, packets, or any other kind of food packaging. The rows on the grid can include the following: product, brand, place of manufacture, amount, ingredients, nutritional information.

Follow-up: Ask the students to call one of the restaurants on the list and ask when it is open. For lower level students you may want to help them plan what to say. Have them report back the next day on what they learned.

BOX 44

Yellow Pages grid

Name	Address	Phone	Special information

Clothing

Students describe their own clothing and that of their classmates. They also have an opportunity to talk about how people dress in their countries. In addition, they can gain useful shopping and clothing care information that they can practice outside the classroom. The study of clothing includes expressing sizes and colors as well as using adjectives, possessives, and numbers.

Clothing descriptions

Students describe and identify clothing.

Time: 10 to 15 minutes
Level: Beginning and up
Main teaching points: Describe clothing
Form and position of adjectives
Organization: Individuals, whole class
Preparation: None

Procedure

1. Describe the clothing of a student in the class and ask the rest of the class to guess who it is. Repeat this several times.
2. Ask the students to describe what each class member is wearing. As they do it, write each student's name and cue words (items of clothing and colors) for describing his clothing on the board or large paper.
3. Give each student a half sheet of paper and ask him to write his name legibly at the top of it. Then collect the papers and redistribute them so that nobody gets his own paper. Review the names of the students so that each person can identify the person he is assigned.
4. Ask each student to write a short description of what that person is wearing.
5. Collect the papers and read them aloud or ask each student to read his paper. Have the rest of the students guess who is being described.

Variations

1. For lower-level students the description might be in the form of a simple list with color and item; for higher-level students it should be in paragraph form.
2. Ask one student to leave the room. Then ask the rest of the students to describe what that person is wearing and write the description on the board. Have the student return and check the accuracy of the description.

Something special

Students talk and write about an item of clothing that is special to them.

Time: 30 to 40 minutes
Level: High beginning and up
Main teaching points: Share personal stories
                       Use past tense
Organization: Individuals, pairs
Preparation: None

Procedure

1. Tell the class about an item of clothing you had once that was very special to you. Tell them what it was, how you got it, and why it was special.
2. Then ask them to think of something they once had which was special to them. Write on the board: *What was it? How or where did you get it? What was special about it?*
3. Divide the class into pairs. Instruct each student to tell his partner about his special item, using the questions as the basis.
4. Divide the class again so that each student has a new partner and have the partners retell about their special item.
5. Finally, have each student write about his special item.

Mail-order catalog matching

In this activity, students match pictures and descriptions of clothing.

Time: 20 minutes
Level: High beginning to intermediate
Main teaching points: Introduce mail-order catalogs
                       Understand descriptions
                       Use correct sequence of adjectives and nouns
Organization: Individuals or small groups

Clothing

Preparation: Cut out a variety of items and their descriptions from
mail-order clothing catalogs, selecting ones with clear descriptions.
Cut the clothing and descriptions apart but keep matching ones in the
same set. Divide the clothing and descriptions into sets of four to ten
items and place each set in a different envelope. The fewer the items
in a set, the easier the task will be. Mix them up in the envelopes. You
will need a set for each group and one or two extras for groups that
finish quickly. If catalogs are not available, you can use any available
clothing pictures and supply your own descriptions.

Procedure

1. Divide the class into small groups.
2. Give each group an envelope and have them match the pictures to
   the descriptions.
3. As the groups finish the task, redistribute the envelopes, making sure
   that the items and descriptions are mixed up.

Variations

1. For lower-level students, write some simpler descriptions of your
   own and reduce the number of items in a set.
2. For more advanced students, increase the number of items in a set as
   well as the complexity of the descriptions.

Follow-ups

1. Give students catalogs to look at. Start with the size, order, and
   information sections. Most catalogs give measurements for sizes.
   Students can use a tape measure to determine their size.
2. Have them look at the order form and accompanying information.
   What information do they need to give? How much is postage? Can
   they return items?
3. Have each student choose something they would like to buy in the
   catalog and practice filling out the order form.
4. A more directed use of the catalogs is to ask students to find
   particular things (a blue shirt, brown socks) and compare prices from
   one catalog to another. If there are stores nearby, students could take
   short lists of items and prices to the stores and compare them.

Real stuff

Students first describe items of clothing and then enter information on a laundry-care chart.

Time: 30 to 40 minutes
Level: High beginning to intermediate
Main teaching points: Read clothing-care labels
Describe clothing
Organization: Individuals, whole class
Preparation: Bring a large bag of clothing from home. Try to bring a variety (children's/adults', men's/women's, winter/summer, long sleeved/short sleeved, old/new, different colors). If possible, bring one item per person. Copy the grid in Box 45 onto the board or a large sheet of paper.

Procedure

1. Have each person reach into the bag and pull out an item of clothing, hold it up, and describe it. The rest of the class can help with the description. Students might also talk about the size (too big, too small) or compare one piece of clothing with another.
2. Using the grid on the board or on the large sheet of paper, make a list of the items in the bag. Have the students dictate the names of the clothing as you write them in the left-hand column of the grid, with the word "Item" above them. Label the second column "Color," the third, "Description," and the fourth, fifth, and sixth, "Wash," "Dry," and "Iron."
3. Ask the students to copy the grid onto their papers.
4. Next ask the students to locate the care labels inside the clothing (the labels that tell how to wash, dry, iron, or dry-clean the item). Have each student look at the item he has taken from the bag and write the information in the appropriate column before passing it on. Students may work together or alone.
5. After they have completed their own grids, ask individual students to complete the large grid as a way to check papers. After all of the information has been entered in the large grid, it can be used as a basis for questions and answers, such as "How do you wash the blue shirt?"

Variation: Lower-level students may be asked to complete only step 1 of the procedure, or use only the first three columns and put a list of colors and words that describe clothing (long sleeved, short sleeved, striped, cotton, synthetic, old, new, collar, buttons, zipper, etc.) on the board. Omit reading the care labels.

⧽⧽⧽→

BOX 45

"Real stuff" laundry grid

Item	Color	Description	Wash	Dry	Iron

Shopping information gap

Students share information in order to complete a list giving information about items purchased.

Time: 15 minutes
Level: Beginning to intermediate
Main teaching points: Vocabulary related to size, color, and price
Ask and answer questions
Organization: Pairs
Preparation: Make enough copies of the form (Box 46) for half of the students to have A and the other half to have B.

Procedure

1. Tell the class that they are going to share information about what a family purchased on a shopping trip. Hand out the A forms to half the class and the B forms to the other half. Explain that each form is missing some information, which the other form has.
2. Go over the form together with the class: the people's names and the heading in each column. Generate the question forms they will need to complete the activity (*What did the mother buy? What size is the shirt? What color is the shirt? How much is the shirt?*)

3. Arrange the students in A–B pairs and tell them to ask each other questions in order to fill in the missing information. They should not look at each others' forms.
4. When a pair has completed the task, they may compare their forms and correct any errors.

Follow-up: Each student can make a list of six items, including color, size, and price. The student then dictates the list to a partner. For additional practice, the student can be assigned to a new partner and repeat the dictation.

BOX 46

Shopping information gap

A

Person	Item	Size	Color	Price
Mother		Medium		$26.99
Father	Suit			$168.32
Daughter		8	Black	
Son	Jacket		Green	

B

Person	Item	Size	Color	Price
Mother	Blouse		Blue	
Father		36 regular	Navy blue	
Daughter	Jeans			$28.50
Son		Small		$29.65

Copyright © Cambridge University Press.

A store

Students locate departments in a store.

Time: 15 to 20 minutes
Level: High beginning to intermediate
Main teaching points: Understand and follow directions
Organization: Individuals, pairs or threes
Preparation: Make one copy of the store plan (Box 47) for each group
   of students. Make one copy of the direction cards (Box 48 on page
   120) for each group of students and arrange them in packs face down
   with card 1 on top. Copy the department name slips (Box 49 on page
   121) and arrange them in random order. These can be kept in
   envelopes and reused.

Procedure

1. Divide the students into pairs and give each group a set of materials
   (plan, direction cards, and department slips).
2. Go over the department slips with the students and talk about what
   clothing they would find in each department.
3. Instruct them to pick up the top card (card 1), read it, and follow the
   directions. Students may take turns reading the directions aloud
   while their partners locate the department, or all the students may
   read the cards. They will place the department slips on the plan to
   locate departments. It may be helpful to do the first card together.
4. When the group has finished, they can go back through the cards
   and check the locations of the departments.

BOX 47

Store plan

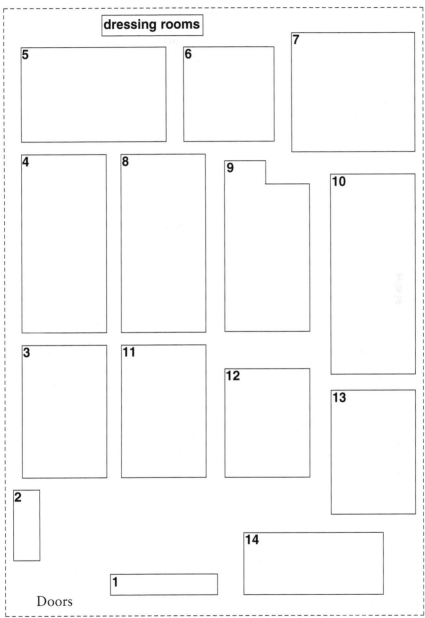

BOX 48

Direction cards

1. The doors are at the front of the store and the dressing rooms are at the back. All directions are from the point of view of a person standing at the doors.	2. The cash registers are near the doors, a little to the right.
3. Children's clothing is at the back of the store, in the back right corner.	4. Men's sweaters are to the right of the cash registers.
5. Customer service and returns are to the left, near the doors.	6. Women's coats and jackets are straight ahead and to the left, after the customer service desk.
7. Women's blouses and sweaters are to the right of women's coats and jackets.	8. Women's accessories (belts, socks, scarves, and jewelry) are to the right of women's blouses and sweaters.
9. Women's underwear is in the back left corner.	10. Women's dresses are between women's coats and jackets and women's underwear, on the left.
11. Men's underwear and socks are to the right of women's accessories.	12. Women's robes, nightgowns, and pajamas are in the back, near the dressing rooms. They are between women's underwear and children's clothing.

BOX 48 (continued)

13. Men's suits and pants are between children's clothing and men's underwear and socks, to the right of shoes.	14. Shoes are to the right of women's skirts and pants.

BOX 49

Department name slips

Cash registers	Customer service and returns
Women's coats and jackets	Women's accessories
Women's dresses	Shoes
Women's underwear	Robes, nightgowns, and pajamas
Children's clothing	Men's sweaters
Men's underwear and socks	Women's skirts and pants
Women's blouses and sweaters	Men's suits and pants

Laundry strips

Students read sentence strips and arrange them in the correct sequence.

Time: 10 to 15 minutes
Level: Beginning to intermediate
Main teaching points: Read directions
                      Sequence events in chronological order
Organization: Pairs
Preparation: Make enough copies of the strips in Box 50 for students to
   share in pairs. Cut them into sets and mix them. Each set can be kept
   separate in an envelope or with a paper clip.

Procedure

1. Review or teach any difficult vocabulary.
2. Divide the students into pairs.
3. Hand out the strips and instruct the students to arrange them in the
   order they would do them.
4. The whole class can check their answers by having individuals write
   the sentences on the board in order.

Follow-up: Have higher-level students work in groups to generate their
   own descriptions of simple processes related to clothing. They should
   cut up the resulting descriptions and exchange them with other
   groups.

BOX 50

Laundry strips

Separate dark and light clothes.

Put the clothes in the washing machine.

Be sure you don't have too many heavy things on one side.

Measure the detergent.

Put the detergent in the washing machine.

Set the water temperature and water level.

Start the machine.

When the machine stops, take out the clothes.

Marketplace

Students "buy" and "sell" items of clothing.

Time: 15 minutes
Level: High beginning to intermediate
Main teaching points: Practice shopping vocabulary
Request items and prices
Practice colors
Organization: Whole class
Preparation: Copy the buying and selling cards (Box 51), making enough for half the class to have a buying card and the other half to have selling cards. For a larger class, make duplicates.

Procedure

1. Give each student a card.
2. Have the students with the selling cards stand up on one side of the room.
3. Tell the remaining students to stand up and talk to the sellers, asking them for items on their lists. If necessary, rehearse the questions before beginning. Buyers and sellers should not show each other their lists, but carry out their transactions orally.
4. Instruct buyers to write down the name of the person from whom they buy each item and the price. Sellers are to mark off the items they have sold.

BOX 51

Buying and selling cards

I want to buy	I want to buy	I want to buy
Brown shoes A red jacket A blue shirt	Orange pajamas A yellow tie Black pants	A purple shirt Blue jeans A blue jacket
I want to buy	**I want to buy**	**I want to buy**
A black hat A red skirt A gold ring	A green sweater A black coat Blue socks	A brown hat A purple shirt White shoes
I want to buy	**I want to buy**	**I want to buy**
A brown suit A gold watch A red sweater	Brown socks A green tie A blue coat	A white shirt A pink blouse Dark blue pants
I want to sell	**I want to sell**	**I want to sell**
Blue jeans for $20 Brown shoes for $63 Orange pajamas for $25	A blue shirt for $21 Black pants for $32 A brown hat for $44	A gold ring for $200 A red jacket for $45 A purple shirt for $15
I want to sell	**I want to sell**	**I want to sell**
Blue socks for $3 A white shirt for $29 A red sweater for $21	White shoes for $58 A gold watch for $280 A blue coat for $135	A brown suit for $200 A green tie for $12 Dark blue pants for $23
I want to sell	**I want to sell**	**I want to sell**
A blue shirt for $28 A red skirt for $33 A black coat for $215	Brown shoes for $53 A green sweater for $5 A pink blouse for $16	A blue jacket for $27 A yellow tie for $16 Brown socks for $4

Clothing survey

Students ask their partners questions about clothing.

Time: 20 minutes
Level: High beginning to intermediate
Main teaching points: Share personal and cultural information concerning clothing
Organization: Pairs, whole class
Preparation: Select one of the clothing surveys (Box 52) and make enough copies so that each student gets one. If you prefer, you may dictate the survey questions.

Procedure

1. Hand out the clothing surveys and go over the questions if necessary.
2. Assign partners and have the students ask their partners the questions in the survey.
3. After they have completed the survey, bring the whole class together again to report on what their partners told them.

Follow-up: Have the students write their own surveys related to clothing.

BOX 52

Clothing survey 1

Ask your partner the following questions about clothing customs in his or her native country.

1. What do men and women wear to work?

2. What do men and women wear for weddings?

3. What do men and women wear when they go out in the evening?

4. What do men and women wear for special holidays?

BOX 52 (continued)

5. What do men and women wear for funerals?

6. What do children wear for school?

Clothing survey 2

Ask your partner the following questions about customs within his or her family.

1. Who buys clothes in your family? Does each person buy them for himself or herself? Does one person buy clothes for other people?

2. Who washes clothes?

3. Who irons clothes?

4. Who repairs torn clothing?

What's my size?

Students take turns dictating information to a partner in order to complete a short text.

Time: 15 to 20 minutes
Level: Intermediate and up
Main teaching points: Learn about differences in conventions for sizing feet
Understand a narrative
Organization: Pairs, whole class
Preparation: Make enough copies of the form (Box 53) for half the students to have story version A and half to have story version B.

Procedure

1. Put the students into pairs.
2. Give version A to one partner in each pair and version B to the other. Explain that they both have the same story but that each version has different words missing. Between the two versions they have the complete story.
3. Have them start at the beginning of the story with person A dictating the first two words to person B. Person B then dictates the next three words to his partner. In this way they alternate dictating parts of the text to their partners until they reach the end of the story.
4. When a pair has completed the task, they should look at their stories together and correct any errors.
5. The whole class together can then discuss differences in conventions for sizing feet.

Variation: Give students copies of form A and read the full version as a dictation. Have the students fill in the blanks.

BOX 53

What's my size story

A

One day _____ _____ _____ a store _____

_____ a pair of _____ . _____ _____

said, "What size _____ _____ _____ wear?" "I'm not

_____," _____ _____ "I think it's about

_____ _____ _____ _____ _____ _____ ."

"A six and a half???" _____ _____ . "Sure. Why are you

_____ _____ ?" " _____ ' _____

_____ _____ take at least a _____ ," _____

_____ . "A 36??" I _____ .

" _____ ' _____ impossible!! If _____ _____

are that big, _____ _____ _____ walk?? That's a _____ ,

_____ _____ _____ ." Then she _____

_____ foot. She showed me _____ _____ .

It said 36. " _____ _____ ' _____ _____ ,"

I said. In the _____ _____

I wear a six _____ _____ _____ ." Then she started

_____ . " _____ I _____ "

she said. "We _____ _____ _____

way to measure _____ _____ . _____ measure

them _____ _____ here."

$\ggg\!\!\rightarrow$

BOX 53 (continued)

B

———— ———— I went to ———— ———————— to buy ————
———————— ———— shoes. The clerk ——————————,
"———————— ———————— shoe do you ——————————?"
"————,' ———— ———— sure, " I said. "———— ————————
————,'———— ———————— a six and a half." ———— ————
———— ———— ———————— ???" she asked. "——————————.
———— ———— ———— so surprised?" "I'm sure you
———————— ———— ———————— ———— 36," she
answered. "———— ———— ??" ———— shouted. "That's
———————————————— !! ———— my feet ————
———————— ————, how can I ———————— ??
————————,'———— ———— boat, not a shoe." ——————————
———— measured my ———————— . ————
———————————————— ———— the measurement. ————
———————— ————. "I don't understand," ————
———————————. ———— ———— United States ————
———————— ———— ———————— and a half."——————————
———— ———————————————to laugh. "Now ————
understand," ———— ——————————. "————have a different
———— ———— ———————————————— foot sizes. We
———————————————— ———————— in centimeters
——————————."

BOX 53 (continued)

Full version

One day I went to a store to buy a pair of shoes. The clerk said, "What size shoe do you wear?" "I'm not sure," I said. "I think it's about a six and a half." "A six and a half???" she asked. "Sure. Why are you so surprised?" "I'm sure you take at least a 36," she answered. "A 36??" I shouted. "That's impossible!! If my feet are that big, how can I walk?? That's a boat, not a shoe." Then she measured my foot. She showed me the measurement. It said 36. "I don't understand," I said. "In the United States I wear a six and a half." Then she started to laugh. "Now I understand," she said. "We have a different way to measure foot sizes. We measure them in centimeters here."

Housing

Housing is an important topic for all students, whether they are looking for a place to live or already have one. They learn to read advertisements in order to find housing. They practice giving and understanding addresses as well as locating them in the community. They practice giving directions inside and outside their homes. In addition, they learn how to describe problems they are having with their homes in order to get them repaired. As students learn about housing, they also learn the names of furniture and rooms. They practice giving descriptions and directions. They have an opportunity to compare housing in their own countries with their classmates'.

Addresses

Students listen and write down addresses from their community.

Time: 10 minutes
Level: Beginning to intermediate
Main teaching points: Understand and write down addresses
$\qquad\qquad\qquad\qquad$ Give information
Organization: Whole class
Preparation: Choose ten addresses that would be useful for the students to know or be able to identify. A phone book may be a useful source.

Procedure

1. Teach students local conventions about addresses before beginning this activity. For example, in the United States, numbers are normally given before street names and street numbers are often grouped by twos when given orally – twenty-one thirty-six for 2136. Another useful convention is that address numbers ascend, east and west, north and south, from particular starting points in each city, with odd and even numbers on opposite sides of the street.
2. Read each address out loud and have the class write it down. Spell street names. Encourage students to ask you to repeat if they have trouble getting the addresses down, rather than looking at a neighbor's paper.

3. When you have completed the dictation, ask individual students to dictate addresses back to you as you write them on the board. This gives students a chance to practice saying addresses as well as to check their papers. This activity can be repeated in several class sessions using different sets of addresses.
4. For additional practice, students can be given addresses to dictate to each other in pairs or to the class.

Variation: For a beginning class, write the street names on the board and practice pronouncing them before beginning the dictation.

Follow-ups

1. Have the students dictate their own addresses to each other.
2. Have the students use city maps to locate the addresses.

Where is it?

Students study a map of the community in which they live and locate important places on the map as well as their own addresses.

Time: 20 to 30 minutes
Level: Beginning and up
Main teaching points: Get acquainted with the community
                               Use maps
                               Give directions
                               Pronounce addresses
Organization: Small groups
Preparation: Have enough maps of your city for three or four students to share one each. A visitors' center may be willing to provide them free of charge. Prepare a list of important places in the community and their locations.

Procedure

1. Go around the class asking students to give their addresses. As students give their addresses, have them spell their street names and say the numbers clearly. You may want to have their classmates write them down.
2. Divide the students into as many groups as there are maps. Locate directions (north, south, east, west) with them as well as major streets. Have the groups work together to locate where the class meets and other important landmarks (rivers, lakes, mountains, parks, malls, schools, etc.).
3. Ask the students to work together in their groups to locate where each member lives and to describe where their homes are.

4. Regroup the students and have each one tell his new group how to get to his house.

Follow-up: Have the students write or tape directions to their homes.

Draw a house*

Students share an element of their own culture with their classmates.

Time: 30 to 40 minutes
Level: Beginning and up
Main teaching point: Share cultural information relating to houses
                      Describe a house
Organization: Pairs, whole class
Preparation: None, unless you choose to supply drawing paper and colored markers. However, this sometimes makes students more self-conscious about their drawing.

Procedure

1. Ask the students to draw a picture of a typical house in their country. It may be one in which they have lived, but that is not necessary. They may draw an interior or exterior view or both.
2. Divide the students into pairs, pairing students from different countries if possible. Have each student describe the house to his partner. In order to encourage students to talk about their drawings, put questions such as the following on the board: *Where is it? How big is it? How many people live in it?* Encourage partners to ask questions as well.
3. After each person has had a chance to tell about the drawing, have the students change partners and tell their new partners about the house. After they finish, reassemble the class and ask what they have learned about houses in other countries.

Follow-up: Higher-level students may write a description of the house they drew. Lower-level students can label their houses (windows, roof, door, etc.) and write a few sentences about them (e.g., "There are four windows").

---

*This activity is not suitable for use in a class where all the students come from the same country.

Room dictation

Students listen to a description of a room and draw what they hear.

Time: 15 to 20 minutes
Level: Beginning and up
Main teaching points: Use furniture vocabulary
Understand and follow directions
Use spatial prepositions
Organization: Whole class
Preparation: None

Procedure

1. Review spatial vocabulary used in the description, such as beside, between, and on.
2. On the board, draw a rectangle to represent a room. Put an arrow above it to indicate that the top of the picture is north. Ask students to copy the picture.
3. Begin reading Room Dictation 1 in Box 54. Pause and repeat as needed.
4. After reading the description, ask two or three students to go to the board and draw the room as the rest of the class check their papers.

Variations

1. For lower-level students, provide copies of the room with the furniture already sketched in. Have them number the furniture and features of the room according to the number of the sentence
2. Have students read room descriptions and draw what they read. Room Dictation 2 (Box 55) or your own description can be used in this way. Check papers by having students draw the resulting picture on the board.
3. Have students work in pairs, with one student dictating while the other draws.

Follow-up: Either passage can be used as a cloze exercise the next day. Write it on a large piece of paper with selected words deleted. Then have students use their drawings from the previous class to fill in and verify words. Students can take turns going up to the paper to fill in words.

⟫→

BOX 54

Room dictation 1

1. The door is in the middle of the south wall.
2. As you walk into the room, the bed is straight ahead, between two windows.
3. To the left of the bed is a bedside table. It has a telephone and a lamp on it.
4. On the left side of the room there is a chest of drawers.
5. To the right of the chest of drawers is a closet door.
6. There are two armchairs near the east wall.
7. The TV set is to the right of the door.
8. To the left of the door there is a dresser.

BOX 55

Room dictation 2

Draw a rectangular room. Put three windows in the middle of the south wall, beside each other. Put the door on the wall opposite the windows, in the right corner. On the east wall in the middle, put a desk. Put a sofa on the south wall in front of the windows. Put a coffee table in front of the sofa. Put an end table and a table lamp to the right of the sofa. Put a TV in the middle of the north wall, to the left of the door. Put a table and six chairs at the west end of the room.

Describe and draw

In this personalized version of Room Dictation (see preceding activity) students describe their own rooms.

Time: 30 to 40 minutes
Level: Beginning and up
Main teaching points: Share personal information
                               Use furniture vocabulary
                               Use conventions for describing rooms
                               Use prepositions
Organization: Pairs
Preparation: None

Procedure

1. Be sure students are familiar with furniture, spatial words, and conventions about describing rooms. To practice this, you may want to do Room Dictation with them first.
2. Ask each student to draw a picture of a room in his house.
3. Divide the class into pairs. Have each student describe his picture to his partner as the partner looks at the drawing. The listener points to specific items in the room as the teller talks about them.
4. Assign new partners and have the class repeat the exercise.
5. Assign new partners. The teller again describes the room he has drawn, but this time must use only words to communicate to his partner, who draws it. His partner cannot see the picture, but must draw it based on what he hears. The teller can make oral corrections to the drawing but cannot touch it. After the drawing is finished, students change roles.

Variation: In a lower-level class, stop after step 4.
Follow-up: The new drawing is passed on to another student, who writes a description based on the picture. All of the pictures are then posted or spread out on a table. Students receive one description each and walk around looking at the drawings until they find the one that corresponds to their description.

Which house?

Students match descriptive words to pictures of houses.

Time: 15 to 25 minutes
Level: Beginning and up
Main teaching points: Describe a place
                               Use adjectives and other descriptive words

》➔

Organization: Individuals or pairs and whole class
Preparation: Collect as many pictures of houses as possible, including
some that are unusual. You can use your own photographs or clip
them from magazines.

Procedure

1. If you have enough pictures for each student to have one, pass them
   out to individuals. Alternatively, students can work in pairs or the
   pictures can simply be put out on a table and students can select one
   without picking it up, with the possibility that more than one
   student will choose the same picture. It is important, however, that
   the student not show or tell others which picture he has chosen.
2. Have each student look at his picture and write down five words
   about it. You may want to model this step by using one picture and
   eliciting descriptive words from the class. The words can be written
   on the board or on a large piece of paper so that everyone can see
   them.
3. Put all the pictures (and a few extras if you have them) in a place
   where everyone can see them. Then have the class work together to
   try to match the pictures with the words.

Follow-up: In a higher-level class an individual or a group can write a
longer description of one of the houses.

Dream house

Students negotiate with the other members of their group in order to
design the perfect house.

Time: 20 to 40 minutes
Level: High beginning and up
Main teaching points: Practice vocabulary for furniture, rooms, and
        buildings
        Use prepositions and other spatial vocabulary
        Negotiate
Organization: Small groups
Preparation: None
Procedure: Ask the students to think about and then draw or write
notes about what they would consider their dream house. Then
divide the class into groups of three. As a group, the students' task
is to design their dream house. They should choose one group
member to draw the house according to the choices the group
makes. Each group can then decide how to present their drawing to
the class.

Residential lease

Pairs of students find the differences between two versions of a lease.

Time: 20 to 30 minutes
Level: High beginning and up
Main teaching points: Understand lease agreements
　　　　　　　　　　　Fill in a lease agreement
Organization: Pairs, whole class
Preparation: Prepare copies of Lease A (Box 56) for half the class and
　copies of Lease B (Box 57 on page 141) for the other half.

Procedure

1. Write the word "lease" on the board. Ask the class to tell you what
　they know about leases. Make notes on the board of what they say.
　Reach a common definition of a lease as used in this activity.
2. Divide the class into pairs, based on level. That is, put lower-level
　students together and higher-level students together.
3. Hand out the papers, but ask the students not to show theirs to their
　partners.
4. Explain that there are two versions of the lease, each slightly
　different. Their task is to find the differences between the two forms
　by reading them back and forth.
5. Have them begin at the top. Have them note the differences as
　they find them. Give the class a time limit of 15 minutes and ask
　them to go over as much of the form as they can in that time.
　Lower-level students will probably be able to complete the top
　half of the form, while higher-level students may complete the
　entire form.
6. When the time is up, partners may compare their forms. The entire
　class may want to discuss the information on the form, comparing it
　with their own leases.

Follow-up: Ask students to bring their own leases and compare them to
　the model.

》》→

BOX 56

Residential lease A

Name of renter: __John Smith__

Apartment address: __1231 Main Street__

Description of apartment:

Number of bedrooms __2__ Number of baths __2__ Number of occupants __3__

Date of occupancy: __June 1__

Term of lease: __12__ months; beginning __June 1__ and ending __May 31__

Monthly rent: __$600__ due on or before the first day of each month.

Utilities furnished: __Water__

Money paid: Security deposit: __$600__

First month's rent: __$600__

Application fee: __$25__

Total: __$1225__

Noise complaint policy

1. First complaint: The manager will send you a letter. A copy of the letter will be placed in your file.
2. Second complaint: The manager will send you another letter.
3. Third complaint: You will have 30 days to move out of your apartment.

House rules

1. Keys will be issued when you move in. You must turn them in when you move out or a $25 replacement fee will be taken out of your deposit.

BOX 56 (continued)

2. Park in your marked space only.
3. Maintenance requests should be called in to the office between 8 and 4. They will be taken care of in the order received unless there is an emergency.
4. Report after-hours emergencies to the emergency number, 555-1243. The following are considered emergencies: no heat, no hot water, water or sewage backup or overflow, severe leak of any kind, electrical failures, fire (dial 911), air conditioning only if the temperature is over 90 degrees.

BOX 57

Residential lease B

Name of renter: ___Jim Smith___

Apartment address: ___1321 Main Street___

Description of apartment:

Number of bedrooms ___1___ Number of baths ___1___ Number of occupants ___2___

Date of occupancy: ___July 1___

Term of lease: ___24___ months; beginning ___July 1___ and ending ___June 30___

Monthly rent: ___$500___ due on or before the first day of each month.

Utilities furnished: **Water, heat**

⟫→

BOX 57 (continued)

Money paid:	Security deposit:	$500
	First month's rent:	$500
	Application fee:	none
	Total:	$1000

Noise complaint policy

1. First complaint: The manager will speak to you. A record of the conversation will be put in your file.
2. Second complaint: The manager will send you a letter and place a copy in your file.
3. Third complaint: You will have 60 days to move out of your apartment.

House rules

1. Keys will be issued when you move in. You must turn them in when you move out or a $20 replacement fee will be taken out of your deposit.
2. Do not park in the spaces marked Visitors.
3. Maintenance requests should be called in to the office between 9 and 5. They will be taken care of in the order received unless there is an emergency.
4. Report after-hours emergencies to the emergency number, 555-1324. The following are considered emergencies: no heat, no hot water, water or sewage backup or overflow, severe leak of any kind, electrical failures, fire (dial 911), air conditioning only if the temperature is over 80 degrees.

Yard sale

Students glean information from classified advertisements for yard sales.

Time: 20 to 30 minutes
Level: High beginning and up
Main teaching points: Use classified advertisements to locate needed items
Scan for information
Organization: Individual, small group, whole class
Preparation: Cut out enough yard sale advertisements for half of the class. Make a list of at least 20 items listed in the ads and write it on the board or on an overhead transparency. In the United States such ads are common in free neighborhood and community newspapers, and yard sales themselves are a useful source of secondhand household items. Box 58 contains samples of such advertisements. In countries where yard sales are not usual, any advertisements containing a list of household items for sale would be suitable.

Procedure

1. Distribute the advertisements to half of the class, giving them to the more advanced students in a multilevel class.
2. Have those students meet together in pairs or small groups to look at their ads and make sure that each person understands his. Meanwhile, have the remaining students each choose three or four items from the list on the board. Draw the grid in Box 59 on page 146 on the board and have them copy it and write their items in the left-hand column.
3. The first group are the "sellers" and the second are the "shoppers." The shoppers walk around the room to the sellers, asking if they have the items on their list. If the seller has one of the items, he dictates the phone number and/or address to the shopper, who records it on the grid.

➤➤➤

BOX 58

Sample yard sale advertisements

YARD SALE! March 14, 7 AM 1234 University Drive, Apt. 84A Toys, clothes, books, file cabinets, microwaves, crib, etc.	TWO-FAMILY YARD SALE Lots of children's toys and clothes, sofa, desk, dishes, and other household items. Saturday, March 14 Begins at 8 AM at 649 McKay Road 555-5436
MULTIFAMILY YARD SALE Antique dining room table and chairs, bedroom furniture, lamps and desk. 320 Elm Street Saturday March 14, 7–12 Rain date: March 21	MOVING SALE Sofa bed, bookshelves, tables, freezer, other furniture, miscellaneous 197 Timberlake Court Saturday, 9–12 No early birds
APARTMENT SALE Everything must go!! Saturday, March 14, 8–2 Leather armchair, coffee table w/matching end tables, chest of drawers, single bed. 422 Old Oxford Road East	YARD SALE: This Saturday, 9–3. Beautiful cherry dining room table with 6 chairs, corner cupboard, lawnmower, crib mattress, and much more. 407 Rutherford Street.

BOX 58 (continued)

HUGE YARD SALE: couch, bunk bed, dresser, carpets, small appliances. Sat., 9–2. 79 Tally Ho Drive.	GARAGE SALE: Outdoor furniture, refrigerator, folding table and chairs. Saturday, 8–4. 307 Camden Avenue.

MOVING SALE

Entertainment center, TV set, sofa, bedroom set, refrigerator, and china. Other household items.
Saturday 3/14, 8–1
567 Spring Forest Rd.

MOVING SALE: 3/14, 8–11.
Floral loveseat, futon, 20-piece china set, bookcase.
6499 Exxon Drive.

NEIGHBORHOOD GARAGE SALE   kitchen table and chairs, clock radios, children's bicycles and more.
988 Park Drive. 9–1, Saturday.
Rain or shine.

LARGE-SCREEN TV, COMPUTER, ANTIQUE FURNITURE (CHEST DRESSER, DESK, CHAIRS), AREA RUGS
Other items too numerous to mention
SATURDAY, MARCH 12, 8–3
Call 555-5476 for directions

BOX 59

Yard sale grid

Item wanted	Phone number/address

Housing survey

Students rank housing priorities.

Time: 20 minutes in class on each of two days
Level: High beginning and up
Main teaching points: Examine and rank housing needs and priorities
Make comparisons
Organization: Individuals, whole class
Preparation: Write the survey items in Box 60 on a large sheet of paper for students to copy. You will later use this paper to record the results of the in-class and out-of-class surveys.

Procedure

1. Ask the students to copy the survey.
2. Ask each person to rate the items from 1 to 8 according to which is most important to him when choosing a place to live.
3. Record the results on the large piece of paper. After price, put 1 and

the number of people in the class who ranked price number 1, then 2 and the number of people who ranked it second. Do the same for each item. To save time, you may only want to record rankings down to 5.

4. Have the students explain their priorities and talk about the results.
5. Then either assign the students to interview another person as homework, or take them to a class where they can interview the members. Have the students discuss the results.

BOX 60

Survey items

Give each of these a number between 1 and 8, where 1 is the most important to you and 8 is the least important.

- Price

- Neighborhood

- Schools

- Location in relation to work/school

- Appearance

- Size

- Yard

- Age of house

Copyright © Cambridge University Press.

Apartment partners

Students find partners by matching information cards and advertisements for rental housing.

Time: 30 to 40 minutes
Level: High beginning and up
Main teaching points: Understand advertisements for housing
Learn vocabulary and abbreviations typical of advertisements for housing
Ask for and give information
Organization: Whole class

»»→

Housing

Preparation: Locate and cut out enough advertisements for apartments in your community for half of your students (local free newspapers are a good source). They can be glued or taped on index cards. For each advertisement, make an index card restating the information in it, such as the following: "I'm looking for a large one-bedroom apartment near the university. I'll be here for 1 year. I can't pay more than $800." These can be as simple or as complex as you like, but each should indicate something specific to one of the advertisements. Samples of advertisement cards are provided in Box 61 and samples of information cards are provided in Box 62 on page 151. Divide the two sets of cards, the ad cards and the information cards, into two separate stacks. Be sure there are enough cards for one advertisement or one information card per student and that each card's pair is also distributed. If there are an odd number of students, two can share one paper. Copy the sample advertisement in Box 61 or put it on an overhead transparency.

Procedure

1. Use the sample advertisements in Box 63 on page 152 for the students to practice reading advertisements, focusing on content vocabulary and abbreviations.
2. Have each student choose a card from one stack or the other.
3. After each student has a card, ask everybody to stand up and walk around, telling others what kind of apartment they have (the ad card people) or what kind of apartment they want (the information card people). When they have found their partners, they should sit down together.
4. Have each pair tell the whole class about the apartment.

Note: If the number of students who attend class varies, you may want to arrange both sets of cards in the same sequence so that when you see how many students are in class, you can pull out the necessary number, half from each stack, and be sure that there is a match for each one.

BOX 61

Advertisement cards

1 BR apt., 5 miles from town. Furnished. Immed. occ. Lrge closets. Pets allowed. $460/mo. Call 555-9195	ARBOR MEADOWS APTS: Minutes from downtown, swimming pool, 1–2 bedrooms, laundry room. 555-8436
Furnished 2 BR, within easy walking distance of downtown. Spacious and bright with fireplace. Call 555-9876	STOP!! CHECK THIS OUT! Efficiency on bus route. $450 a month, heat and air included. 555-8133
2 BR apt. All utilities except telephone provided. $890 per month with one month security deposit. 3 months minimum lease. No smokers or pets. Parking provided. Call 555-9364.	VERY CLEAN 1 BEDROOM APT. On bus route. Prefer non-smoker, nondrinker. No pets, please. $500 a month plus deposit. Includes utilities. 555-2183

⟫→

BOX 61 (continued)

LUXURY 1 BEDROOM. Five minutes from shopping center. Hardwood floors, free heat. $650/month. 555-7154

3 bedroom condo. Newly painted, quiet, top floor. Appliances. Available Aug. 16. $790. Call Hope Management, 555-4590

FOUR BEDROOM HOUSE IN TOWN. Every appliance included. Carpeted, central air, gas heat, study, ceiling fans, garage with work space. $1,500 per month. 555-8012

1,300-square-foot house at Colony Lake. 2 BR, 2 BA, plus patio. Fireplace. Dishwasher, washer and dryer hookups. On bus line. Good schools. Great family neighborhood. $850/ month. Available now. 555-5338

2 BEDROOM APARTMENT: large eat-in kitchen, washer and dryer connections, 6 miles from town. Country living at its best. No pets. $500 per month. 1 year lease. Call 753-9330

AVAILABLE NOW: Fully furnished, spacious downtown apartment. No parking. Balcony overlooking Main Street.

BOX 62

Information cards

I'm looking for a small apartment. I have a dog. I need to move right now.	I need a two bedroom apartment near downtown. I like to swim.
My family needs a two bedroom apartment for two months. I work downtown and we don't have a car.	I live alone and am looking for a small apartment. I can't pay more than $450 a month. I take the bus to work.
We are looking for a two bedroom apartment. We don't smoke. We have a car. We will be staying here for 1 year.	I don't smoke or drink. I'm looking for a small apartment. I can pay a maximum of $550 a month.
I work at the shopping center and prefer to walk to work. I can pay up to $650 a month.	I'm looking for a quiet apartment. I don't have any appliances. I need to move in the middle of August.
I'm looking for a four bedroom house with a garage and appliances. I can pay as much as $1,500 per month.	I need two bedrooms and two bathrooms. I'd like a patio so my children can play outside. It must be near good schools and a bus line.
I need a two bedroom apartment. I like to live outside of town. I have my own washer and dryer.	I don't have a car. I want to live downtown. I'd like to have a balcony for my plants.

)))→

BOX 63

Sample advertisement

2 br apt near bus line and shopping.

Stove and refrigerator.

Immediate occupancy.

555-7235

$800

First, last, security.

Whose problem is it?

Students list maintenance and safety problems in their apartments and decide who is responsible.

Time: 15 to 20 minutes
Level: High beginning and up
Main teaching points: Gain cultural awareness of potential maintenance
and safety problems
Describe a problem
Organization: Whole class, small groups
Preparation: None

Procedure

1. Ask the students to tell about problems in their apartments. Make a list on the board.
2. Divide the class into small groups and ask them to divide the problems on the list into two categories: those for which the landlord is responsible and those for which the tenant is responsible.
3. Bring the class together again to compare their results.
4. The teacher gives any information she has available about the local situation, and refers the students to other possible sources of information.

Follow-up: Have the students seek out further information concerning their local situation from native speakers, tenants associations, citizen advice bureaus, housing offices, and so on, and report back to the class.

Repair split dialogue

Students rehearse conversations requesting help with household repairs.

Time: 10 to 15 minutes
Level: High beginning and up
Main teaching point: Request help with household problems
Organization: Pairs, whole class
Preparation: Prepare copies of the Student A dialogue cue card for half of the class and enough copies of the Student B cue card for the other half (Box 64).

Procedure

1. Give out Student A cards to half the class and Student B cards to the other half.
2. Have the As sit together and the Bs sit together. They should look through their papers, making sure they understand everything and discussing any questions they may have.
3. Divide the class into pairs, with one A and one B in each. Ask the students not to show their cards to their partners.
4. Explain that they have been given different roles in the same dialogue and that their job is to read the dialogue aloud, alternating roles. Explain further that at several points in the dialogue one or the other student will be given options as to how to continue the dialogue. In this case the student's job is to listen carefully to the preceding conversation and select the most appropriate continuation. At the beginning of the dialogue Student A has a free choice as to which cue he selects.
5. Have the students read through the dialogue several times aloud in pairs, choosing different options.
6. Have several pairs read through their dialogues for the whole class and discuss the appropriateness of the options they have chosen.

Follow-ups

1. Have the students construct their own split dialogues.
2. Have each student write a note to his landlord describing a problem in his apartment.

⫸→

BOX 64

Repair split dialogue

Student A cue card	Student B cue card
A. The electricity went off. My bathroom sink is overflowing. I don't have any heat.	A.
B.	B. I'll call a furnace repair person. I'll call a plumber. I'll call an electrician.
A. When will it be fixed?	A.
B.	B. Next year. Tomorrow morning. A week from Monday.
A. I have another problem, but it isn't an emergency.	A.

BOX 64 (continued)

B.	B. Oh? What is it?

A.
 	
My window won't stay open.
The paint in my bedroom is
  peeling.
There are cockroaches in my
  kitchen.
	A.

B.	B. I'll call an exterminator. I'll call a carpenter. I'll call a painter.
A. Thanks a lot.	A.

Health

Health is a topic of vital interest and relevance to all students. At some time during their stay, they or members of their family are likely to have encounters with the medical system.

Students learn to name body parts and symptoms, how to make a doctor's appointment, what to say at the doctor's office, how to fill in medical forms, and how to read labels on medicines.

Free materials are available from doctors' and dentists' offices, pharmacies, public health facilities, and school and workplace clinics. These include sample registration forms, immunization information, treatment of common problems such as headaches or backaches, and health insurance information. Home health and first-aid materials as well as medicine labels are easily available.

Body drawing

Each student draws and labels a part of the body.

Time: 20 minutes
Level: Beginning to intermediate
Main teaching points: Name body parts
                                   Follow instructions
Organization: Individuals, whole class
Preparation: None

Procedure

1. On a blackboard or a large piece of paper, draw a circle near the top and label it "head."
2. Name another body part, perhaps "neck," and ask a student to draw it and label it.
3. Continue to name body parts in random order and call on students.

Variation: In a low beginning class it is probably best to name body parts in order rather than randomly.
Follow-up: After the drawing is completed, students may go up one at a time to name and erase a body part and label.

Getting in shape

Students arrange themselves in the form of a body.

Time: 10 minutes
Level: Beginning to intermediate
Main teaching points: Name body parts
                          Understand health problems
                          Negotiate
                          Follow instructions
Organization: Individuals, whole class
Preparation: Make a set of body parts strips as in Box 65. For a large class, prepare more than one set using a different color of paper for each set.

Procedure

1. Clear an area of the room or use a corridor or other open space.
2. Distribute the body parts strips, one per student. If there are fewer students than the number of strips, simply remove some strips.
3. Tell the students to stand up and, using the names on their strips, arrange themselves in the shape of a body. Each person must tell the others which part he has and negotiate with them where to stand. This should be done orally, without showing their strips to their classmates.
4. Read out the getting in shape problems in Box 66 in random order and have the students return to their seats when they hear a problem related to their body part.

Variations

1. In a large class, first divide the students into smaller groups based on the color of their strips.
2. The same strips can be placed in order on a wall or table.

»→

BOX 65

Getting in shape: body parts

Head	Neck	Shoulder
Arm	Wrist	Hand
Chest	Stomach	Leg
Ankle	Foot	Toe
Finger	Ear	

BOX 66

Getting in shape: problems

I have a headache.	I have chest pains.
I have a sore neck.	I have a stomachache.
I hurt my shoulder.	I broke my leg.
I broke my arm.	I turned my ankle.
I sprained my wrist.	My foot is asleep.
I have arthritis in my hand.	I broke my toe.
I sprained my finger.	I have an earache.

Body part bingo

Students play bingo with names of body parts.

Time: 30 to 45 minutes
Level: Intermediate
Main teaching points: Understand definitions
Follow directions
Organization: Whole group
Preparation: None

Procedure

1. First, read each description in Box 67 to the class and ask the students to identify the body part it describes.
2. On the board, draw a grid with twenty-five boxes, five horizontal and five vertical, as in a bingo grid. Instruct the students to copy the grid, making each box large enough to write in a word.
3. Dictate the words in the list in Box 67, telling the students to write one word in each box in any order. Model this with the grid on the board. Explain to the students that you are going to read a description of each word. As you read the description, the students will mark a small X in the corner of the box with the matching word. The object of the game is to get five squares in a row, vertically, horizontally, or diagonally. When a student gets five in a row, he should call out "Body!!"
4. Begin the game by reading the descriptions in any order. As you read the descriptions, mark the list to keep track of which ones you have given. When a student announces that he has won, have him read back the words he has marked. The game can be repeated once or twice, with the students marking the squares in different ways, as with an O or a horizontal line.

Variation: For a lower-level class, write the words on the board rather than dictating them. Omit step 1 and read the words themselves, rather than their descriptions.

BOX 67

Bingo words and descriptions

Elbow	This joint lets you bend your arm.
Mouth	You use this to talk and to eat.
Knee	This joint lets you bend your leg.
Lungs	You use these when you breathe. They are inside your chest. When you breathe, they fill up with air.
Arm	This is between your shoulder and your hand.
Heart	This muscle pumps blood around your body.
Neck	This connects your head to the rest of your body.
Ear	You use these to hear.
Leg	You have two of these. You use them to walk. The knee is between the top part and the bottom part.
Eyes	You use these to see.
Teeth	You use these to chew your food. They are inside your mouth.
Foot	Each of these has five toes.
Fingers	You have five of these on each hand.
Toes	You have five of these on each foot.
Hand	You use these to hold things. Each one has five fingers.
Ankle	This joint is between your leg and your foot.
Wrist	This joint is between your arm and your hand.

⫸→

BOX 67 (continued)

Blood	Your heart pumps this around your body.
Larynx	This is also called your voice box.
Trachea	This is used in breathing to carry air to your lungs. It is also called your windpipe.
Shoulder	This joint lets you raise your arm. It is between your arm and the rest of your body.
Hair	This covers your head and keeps it warm.
Nose	You use this to smell and to take air into your body.
Chest	This is the top part of your body. Inside of it are your heart and lungs.
Brain	This controls all the actions of your body. You use it to think and remember.

Three-part appointment gap

Students ask their partners for and record missing information about medical appointments.

Time: 20 to 30 minutes
Level: Intermediate
Main teaching points: Understand appointment information
                         Pronounce correctly
                         Ask and answer questions
Organization: Groups of three, whole class
Preparation: Make enough copies of the forms in Box 68 for each student to have one form (A, B, or C).

Procedure

1. If necessary, review days, dates, times, and medical problems.
2. Organize the class into threes. Hand out Form A to one member of each group, Form B to another, and Form C to a third. Explain to the students that for the purpose of this exercise they are three secretaries working in a clinic. Each of the secretaries has only part of the information he needs relating to patient appointments and must ask the others for the remaining information.
3. Have the entire class look at and pronounce the names of the patients. Be sure the students understand how the chart is organized. If necessary, review or rehearse the questions they need to ask to elicit the information that is missing.
4. Have the students ask each other (without looking at each others' papers) for the information missing from their papers.
5. When the groups have finished, put the chart on the board. Either have individuals come to the board to fill in the chart or have them dictate the information to you.

Variation: The two right-hand columns of the grid can be masked to limit the task for beginners.

⋙➔

BOX 68

Health appointments information gap

Form A

Name	Day	Time	Date	Problem
Mr. Lee	Tuesday			Backache
Mrs. Lee			2/3	
Miss Jones		2:30		
Mr. Ritter	Friday			Sore throat
Ms. Little				
Mrs. Johnson	Friday	10:45		

Form B

Name	Day	Time	Date	Problem
Mr. Lee		9:45		
Mrs. Lee	Thursday			Earache
Miss Jones			2/2	
Mr. Ritter		3:00		
Ms. Little	Monday			Stomachache
Mrs. Johnson			2/4	

BOX 68 (continued)

Form C				
Name	**Day**	**Time**	**Date**	**Problem**
Mr. Lee			2/1	
Mrs. Lee		11:15		
Miss Jones	Wednesday			Flu
Mr. Ritter			1/28	
Ms. Little		4:15	1/31	
Mrs. Johnson				Headache

Copyright © Cambridge University Press.

Medicine directions

Students write down the essential information from a medicine label.

Time: 20 to 30 minutes
Level: Beginning to intermediate
Main teaching point: Understand information on a medicine label
Organization: Whole class
Preparation: Copy the label forms (Box 69), making enough copies of Label A for higher-level students and of Label B for lower-level students.

Procedure

1. Hand out the label forms. Be sure that all of the students understand the vocabulary on the labels, paying particular attention to the abbreviation Rx for prescription.
2. Read the text "label information" (Box 70 on page 167) to the students, having them write the missing information in the appropriate spaces.

Follow-up: Ask students to bring in containers of their own medications. Have them fill in additional blank label forms using the information from their own medicine containers. More advanced students may dictate them to each other.

>>>→

BOX 69

Pharmacy label forms

Label A

PROFESSIONAL PHARMACY	
RX Number	Telephone number
Instructions	Warnings
Refills	

Label B

PROFESSIONAL PHARMACY	
RX Number	Telephone number
Instructions	Warnings
Take _____ tablets now.	Take with food **YES/NO**
Then take _____ tablet	Finish all this medication **YES/NO**
every _____ hours	May cause drowsiness **YES/NO**
Refills	
YES/NO	

BOX 70

Label information text

The telephone number of the pharmacy is 555-8735. The prescription number is 9466013281. You should take two tablets now and then take one tablet every six hours. There are no refills on this prescription. Remember to finish all of the medication. Take it on an empty stomach one hour before or two to three hours after a meal. In some individuals, this medication may cause drowsiness.

Copyright © Cambridge University Press.

First aid

Students discuss common first-aid problems and their solutions.

Time: 40 minutes
Level: Intermediate and up
Main teaching points: Learn how to deal with common first-aid
　　　　　　　　　　　problems
　　　　　　　　　　　Learn health vocabulary
Organization: Pairs or small groups and whole class
Preparation: Make enough copies of the questionnaire in Box 71 for each student; but do not include the answers from the end of the box. Put the answers on an overhead or large sheet of paper.

Procedure

1. Divide the class into pairs or small groups and distribute copies of the questionnaire.
2. Have the students read and discuss each problem and their possible solutions. They should try to reach consensus on each one.
3. When the groups have finished discussing all the problems, ask them to share their answers to the first problem with the whole class. Encourage discussion among the groups.
4. Reveal the first answer and discuss it. Do the same with the other problems. If the students disagree with the answers that are given, suggest that they investigate further at the public library or with health professionals.

Follow-up: Have students suggest further health problems and discuss solutions.

⠀⠀⠀**≫→**

BOX 71

First-aid questionnaire

Choose the best answer for each question.

1. A friend has a deep bleeding cut on her arm. You should:
   a. Tie something around her arm to cut off the blood supply
   b. Take her to the doctor's office
   c. Put a thick dressing on it
   d. Put pressure on it with a clean gauze pad

2. Your fourteen-year-old son is playing football. He knocks a tooth out of his mouth. You should:
   a. Place the tooth back in his mouth and call the dentist
   b. Place the tooth in a glass of milk and call the dentist
   c. Wrap the tooth in gauze and call the dentist
   d. Place the tooth in a cup of ice and call the dentist

3. You find a three-year-old child eating aspirins. You don't know how many she has eaten, but you know it is more than five. You should:
   a. Not let the child sleep for six hours and watch her carefully
   b. Take the child to the nearest hospital
   c. Make the child vomit
   d. Give the child milk to dilute the aspirin

4. Your neighbor comes to your house complaining that he has something in his eye. You can see a small piece of wood under the lower eyelid. You should:
   a. Try to remove the wood with your finger
   b. Hold his eye open and pour water into it
   c. Tell him to keep his eye closed and put a patch over it
   d. Tell him to rub his eye to get the wood out

BOX 71 (continued)

5. You burn your hand badly on a hot pot. It is red and painful. Blisters are beginning to form. You should:
   a. Apply butter or some other oily substance to the burn
   b. Place your hand in ice water
   c. Go to the hospital immediately
   d. Apply a cool wet cloth to the area

Answers

1. a. No, because you may damage the entire arm. b. No, because it's too slow. c. No, because it will bleed through the dressing. d. Yes. It reduces the blood going to a localized area.

2. a. Yes, but only if the person is old enough not to swallow it. In this way there is a good chance that the tooth can be saved and reimplanted. b. This is the second-best choice. It would be the best one for a young child. c. No, because the tooth will dry out and die. d. No, because the cold temperature may damage blood vessels.

3. a. No, because the aspirin is still in her system. b. No, because it takes too long. c. Yes, because it gets the aspirin out of her system. This is not, however, the best solution for all poisons. d. No, as in a.

4. a. No, because you may scratch the eye. b. Yes. c. No, because the wood is still in his eye. d. No, as in a.

5. a. No. This can cause infection. b. No, because this treats too general an area and may damage the arm. c. No, because it is not that serious. d. Yes.

Heimlich maneuver

Students learn to perform the Heimlich maneuver.

Time: 20 minutes
Level: High beginning to intermediate
Main teaching points: Learn to perform the Heimlich maneuver
　　　　　　　　　　　　Learn health vocabulary
　　　　　　　　　　　　Follow instructions
Organization: Pairs
Preparation: Make one copy of the picture sheet and one of the Heimlich instruction sheet for each pair (Box 72).

Procedure

1. Tell the class that they are going to learn about a first-aid technique that has saved many lives.
2. Be sure that students understand the following vocabulary: *thumb, fist, abdomen, neck, waist, victim, breathe, cough, choke,* and *continue.*
3. Divide the class into mixed level pairs. Hand out a picture sheet to the lower-level student (A) and an instruction sheet to the higher-level student (B). They should not show each other their papers.
4. Have student B read the instructions aloud to student A, while he numbers the pictures from 1 to 6 in sequence. When they have completed this task, have them check the numbering together.

Follow-up: Have the students read the instructions aloud as two students demonstrate the maneuver.

BOX 72

Heimlich maneuver pictures

STUDENT A: Pictures

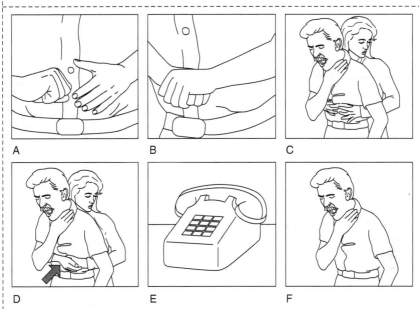

A B C

D E F

Student B: Instructions for Heimlich Maneuver

1. You see a person who cannot breathe or cough.
   He is holding his neck.
   Ask the person if he is choking.
2. If the person can't answer, send someone to call the local
   emergency number.
3. Then stand behind the victim and put your arms around his waist.
4. Make a fist. Place the thumb side of your fist in the middle of
   the victim's abdomen.
5. Hold your fist with other hand.
6. Press your fist with quick upward thrusts into the abdomen.
7. Continue until the victim starts breathing or help arrives.

Listen and say

Students take turns in a sequence of dialogs.

Time: 10 minutes
Level: High beginning to intermediate
Main teaching points: Give advice
                                 Follow directions
Organization: Whole class
Preparation: Copy Box 73 and cut the strips apart. Put them in an envelope and mix them up.

Procedure

1. Have each student draw a strip from the envelope. If there are fewer students than strips, some may take more than one. If there are more students than strips, they can share.
2. Explain that this is a listening and speaking activity in which each person must listen to what the preceding person says. When he hears the cue indicated on the strip ("When you hear . . . "), he says his part. Write an example from one of the strips on the board. Point out the part that says, "When you hear. . . . ?" Give the cue on the board and have the class respond. Tell the class to speak loudly and clearly so that the next person can hear and understand them.
3. Begin with the "start" person. Usually the first time through somebody gets mixed up. If that happens, you will get to the end without everybody having a turn. Go back to the beginning and start again if there is a problem. Students may help their neighbors. If you want to do it again, redistribute the strips.

BOX 73

Listen and say strips

Start: **I cut my finger.**	When you hear "throat," say **Drink some tea with honey.**
When you hear "my finger," say **Wash it and put on a Band-Aid.**	When you hear "honey," say **I have a rash.**
When you hear "Band-Aid," say **I burned my hand.**	When you hear "rash," say **Don't scratch it.**
When you hear "hand," say **Put cold water on it.**	When you hear "scratch it," say **I broke my leg.**
When you hear "water on it," say **I have chills.**	When you hear "leg," say **Go to the Emergency Room.**
When you hear "chills," say **Go to bed and keep warm.**	When you hear "room," say **I sprained my ankle.**
When you hear "warm," say **I have a headache.**	When you hear "ankle," say **Stay off of it.**
When you hear "headache," say **Take some aspirin.**	When you hear "off of it," say **I have high blood pressure.**
When you hear "aspirin," say **I have a sore throat.**	When you hear "pressure," say **Take it easy.** **The end**

Rotating brainstorm

Groups of students brainstorm and write solutions to medical problems
and then read and add to those of other groups.

Time: 20 to 30 minutes
Level: Intermediate and up
Main teaching points: Suggest solutions to medical problems
　　　　　　　　　　　　Share cultures
　　　　　　　　　　　　State opinions
Organization: Groups of three to five, whole class
Preparation: Prepare sheets of chart paper with the following headings:
　Sore throat, Black eye, Fever, Nosebleed, Headache, Burns, Earache.
　The number of topics can be adjusted to accommodate the number
　of students.

Procedure

1. Post chart papers on the wall around the room, spaced so that each
   group has room to work.
2. Divide the class into groups of three to five. Assign each group
   to one of the papers. Give the groups 5 minutes to brainstorm
   possible remedies to the problem if no doctor or drugstore is
   available.
3. Rotate the groups, with each going on to the next sheet. Give them
   2 minutes to read and discuss what the previous group wrote. Then
   allow an additional 2 minutes to add their own suggestions. They
   should not change or correct the notes of the previous group.
4. Continue to rotate the groups until each group has contributed to all
   the papers. At this point, ask each group to read to the whole class
   the contents of their final chart. Discuss the solutions.

Medical form

Students fill in a medical form based on information brought to them by a group member.

Time: 30 minutes
Level: Beginning and up
Main teaching points: Fill in a medical form
          Read and answer questions
Organization: Groups
Preparation: Fill in a master copy of the New Patient Information form (Box 74) for a fictitious person, using a local address, phone number, and so on. Make two copies of this master to post on the wall and an extra copy per group, for checking at the end of the activity. Make a copy of the blank form for each group.

Procedure

1. Post the master copies where the students cannot see them directly from their seats.
2. Divide the class into groups.
3. Give one copy of the blank form to each group.
4. Ask each group to choose a "runner," that is, a person who will go to the master form and retrieve information. The rest of the group will take turns recording the information on the blank form. Point out to the groups that there are three identical masters posted on the wall, and the runner can go to whichever master is closest to the group. When the activity begins, the runner goes to the master and returns with information for the group. He may not write the information; instead, he must dictate it to his group. He may return to the master form as many times as necessary. The group is finished when they have all the information required on their form.

Variation: Ask lower-level groups or classes to include only the information above line A, and intermediate ones only the information above line B.

➤➤➤

BOX 74

New patient information form

Patient's name _____
            (last)   *(first)*   *(middle)*

Patient's address_____
    number/ street   */ apt. /*   *city*   /   *state*   /   *zip*

Home phone _____ Date of birth_____/_____/_____

age _____ SS# _____

(Line A) *

Employed by_____

Employer's address_____

Spouse's name_____

Employed by_____

Method of payment: Cash or check_____

Insurance Company_____

Medical history

Are you taking any medication? If so, what?_____

Are you allergic to any medication? If so, what? _____

(Line B) *

Have you had any major surgery?

Have you ever been treated for _____ heart disease, _____

cancer, _____ asthma, _____ diabetes, _____alcoholism,

_____ high blood pressure, _____depression

If you answered yes to any of these, please give details:

BOX 74 (continued)

Have you been treated for other serious diseases?

Is there a history in your family of _____ heart disease, _____ cancer, _____ asthma, _____ diabetes, _____ alcoholism, _____ high blood pressure, _____ depression

If you answered yes to any of these, please give details:

Community options

Students work together to collect information about health options in their community.

Time: This activity takes place over a number of class periods, during which students report on the information they have collected. The initial setup of the project will take about 30 minutes.
Level: Intermediate and up
Main teaching points: Learn about local health options
Locate information
Summarize and report
Organization: Mixed-level groups
Preparation: None

Procedure

1. Have the students brainstorm a list of community health-care options (public clinics, private clinics, emergency and urgent-care facilities). Add any that you think are important that have not been included. List them on the board. With your students, identify those that are most useful.
2. On a large sheet of paper, write the list in the left-hand column. Across the top, list the following items: phone number, address, hours, days. Who can go there? What kinds of problems are treated? Payment? Are appointments needed? Comments. In order to save space, abbreviated forms of the questions can be used, but be sure the students understand what they mean.
3. Look at the grid with the students. Tell them that their task is to contact these places and get the information required on the grid.
4. Divide the class into groups and assign a health-care option to each group. The groups then meet and decide how to accomplish the task.
5. After the students have had time to collect the information outside class, have each group write the results of their investigation in the spaces on the grid.
6. Ask the rest of the class to add their comments about those facilities with which they are familiar.
7. Have the groups meet and expand the results of their investigations into a narrative about their facility. During the process of writing, give students an opportunity for review and editing.
8. Give copies to each student in the class. Extra copies can be provided for friends or family members and for new students.

Work

Finding a job is the first priority for many adult language learners. They need to learn the expectations, both cultural and linguistic, of job seekers and workers. Even for those who do not plan to work in the new country, the working lives they left behind are important to their sense of who they are and provide a departure point for comparison with the new country. In this unit students consider different kinds of jobs and the qualifications required for them. They learn how to get a job and what kinds of behaviors and problems occur at work.

What can you do?

Students list and analyze their work-related skills.

Time: 20 to 30 minutes
Level: Beginning and up
Main teaching point: Analyze personal work-related skills
Organization: Individuals, whole class
Preparation: None

Procedure

1. Tell the class that you are going to think together about what skills are needed for working. As the members of the class brainstorm, write the suggestions on the board. You may want to begin by writing a few of your own skills on the board (e.g., I can use a computer; I work well with other people).
2. Ask the students individually to make a list of the work skills they have.
3. Post the following list of jobs on the board and ask the students to add other jobs to it:
   Construction worker   Secretary
   Nurse   Travel agent
   Cook   Teacher
4. Ask the students to match their skills with possible jobs.
5. Have each student choose the job that would be most interesting to him and write about it.

Salary dictation

Students write a dictation about jobs and salaries in their new country.

Time: 15 to 20 minutes
Level: Beginning and up
Main teaching points: Get an overview of salaries
Listen and record information
Organization: Individuals, whole class
Preparation: Find current salary information for people working in your country. Make a dictation such as that given in Box 75 with representative jobs and pay. Make a copy of the blank grid Box 76 for each student, or have them copy the grid from the board.

Procedure

1. Tell the class that they are to write down the information you give them on their grid.
2. Read the information for each person in Box 75 (or your own local version of it) using full sentences. Spell names and occupations if needed and repeat as necessary.
3. Have individuals or pairs come to the board to write the information they have written so that all the students can check their papers.
4. Look at the dictated information with the students. How do salaries in their new country compare with those in their home countries?

Variation: In a lower-level class, write the names and occupations on the board; dictate just the numbers.

BOX 75

Salary dictation

Name	Age	Job	Pay
Christopher	37	Autoworker	$45,000
Sylvia	34	Violinist	$37,500
Bill	50	President	$200,000
Alanis	23	Singer	$22,000,000
Michael	28	Teacher	$24,500
Jane	35	Saleswoman	$24,000
Sandra	60	Nurse	$33,000
Mary	46	Baker	$11,000

Copyright © Cambridge University Press.

BOX 76

Salary dictation blank grid

Name	Age	Job	Pay

Copyright © Cambridge University Press.

What's my job?

Students select mystery occupations and their classmates guess which one they have chosen.

Time: 20 to 30 minutes
Level: Beginning and up
Main teaching points: Learn words for occupations
Practice yes/no questions
Organization: Groups, whole class
Preparation: Write the occupations in Box 77 on separate slips of paper and put them in an envelope.

Procedure

1. Explain to the students that they will take turns selecting a "secret" occupation from the envelope. The other students will try to guess their choice by asking 20 yes/no questions.
2. Brainstorm questions they could ask that would help them to identify specific occupations, such as "Do you work outdoors?" or "Do you look after people?" In a large class you may wish to break the class into groups so that the students have more chance to ask questions.

Variation: In lower-level classes you may want to limit your students to fewer occupations.

BOX 77

Occupations

Salesclerk	Taxi driver	Pilot
Truck driver	Dentist	Auto mechanic
Actor	Teacher	Secretary
Electrician	Bricklayer	Singer
Doctor	Librarian	Nurse
Factory worker	Cashier	Scientist
Banker	Carpenter	Police officer
Housewife/	Journalist	Translator
housohusband	Plumber	Lawyer

Copyright © Cambridge University Press.

How do they rank?

Students rank jobs according to given criteria.

Time: 20 minutes
Level: High beginning and up
Main teaching points: Share cultural information regarding jobs
Comparisons
Organization: Individuals, groups, whole class
Preparation: None

Procedure

1. Ask the class to brainstorm a list of ten jobs.
2. Then ask each student to rank the jobs according to each of the following criteria. In each case, 1 will be the lowest rank and 10 will be the highest.
   • Status
   • Pay
   • Level of education
   • Appeal
3. Divide the class into groups. If possible, the members of the group should be from the same or a related culture. The group then tries to come to a definitive ranking according to their culture's views.
4. Regroup the students so that there are (as far as possible) representatives from different cultures within each group. Have them compare and discuss their rankings.
5. Have the groups report back to the whole class anything that surprised or that particularly interested them in the discussion.

Stress ratings

Students rate jobs according to the level of stress they involve.

Time: 30 minutes
Level: High beginning and up
Main teaching points: Examine the relationship between work and
stress
Give and support opinions
Make comparisons
Negotiate
Organization: Individuals, pairs, groups, whole class
Preparation: Write the following job names on numbered sheets of
paper and post around the room: air traffic controller, teacher,
secretary, mother, coach, waitperson, police officer, doctor, lawyer,
and salesperson. Draw the grid in Box 78 on the board.

Procedure

1. Make sure that the students understand the meaning of each job.
2. Ask the students individually to select the three they think are most
stressful and the one they think is least stressful.
3. As they finish, pair them and give them 10 minutes to repeat the task
as a pair. They must reach agreement on all their choices. If
necessary you may also have a group of three students.
4. As the pairs finish, double them up to make groups of four or five
and have them repeat the task one last time.
5. As the groups finish, ask each group to record their choices on the
grid on the board, using plus signs for the three they decided were
most stressful and a minus sign for the one they decided was least
stressful.
6. Discuss with the whole class choices where there are differences
between the groups.

BOX 78

Stress ratings grid

JOB	Group A	Group B	Group C	Group D
Air traffic controller				
Teacher				
Secretary				
Mother				
Coach				
Waitperson				
Police officer				
Doctor				
Lawyer				
Salesperson				

Copyright © Cambridge University Press.

Job advertisements

Students scan job advertisements for specific information.

Time: 40 minutes (this may be extended or decreased by giving more or fewer ads to each group)
Level: High beginning and up
Main teaching points: Use newspaper advertisements to learn about jobs
Scan for specific information
Learn vocabulary specific to job advertisements
Organization: Individuals, mixed-level groups, whole class

Preparation: Collect classified advertisements for jobs from a local newspaper. Examples of such advertisements are shown in Box 79. You should have approximately one per student. If possible, choose advertisements that are relevant to your students.

Procedure

1. Pose the question: What kind of information can you find in a job advertisement? Take their answers and make a grid on the board, such as the one shown in Box 80.
2. Divide the students into mixed-level groups. Give each group a large sheet of paper and ask the groups to copy the grid onto their paper.
3. Pass out three or four advertisements to each group. Have each student take responsibility for finding a particular kind of information from each advertisement and for filling in the grid. Have additional advertisements available in case some groups finish the task before others do.
4. Have the groups check through their charts together and then post them so that the rest of the class can see them.
5. Finally, have students choose the job from all those on the posted grids that would be best for them and explain why, either orally or in writing.

Variation: In mixed level groups, the teacher may choose to assign tasks as follows: lower-level students, phone number, pay, and hours categories; higher-level students, the description, requirements, and location categories.

Follow-ups

1. Have the students make a list of the skills they have that would help them to do the job they selected. Then ask them to write letters applying for the job.
2. The students may share their letters with other group members and ask for suggestions as to any additional skills they have that would also be useful.

BOX 79

Job advertisements

Painters needed	No nights!
Experience necessary Transportation and phone required Call Donald Howard 555-7397	Waitperson needed for breakfast or lunch Benefits available Full or part time Sunshine Cafe 555-8181
Experienced nurses needed. Full and part time. Hospital contracts available. Up to $31 per hour plus benefits. Call City Hospital 555-9246.	Taxi Drivers needed. Flexible hours. Minimum 2 years driving experience. Earn up to $500 per week. 555-2359

BOX 80

Job ads grid

Description	Requirements	Pay	Hours	Location	Phone numbers

How to get a job

Students interview classmates and others who have jobs in order to gain job search skills.

Time: 30 to 40 minutes
Level: High beginning and up
Main teaching points: Gain job search skills
                          Give advice
                          Ask and answer questions
Organization: Groups, whole class
Preparation: Post two or three large sheets of paper around the room with the heading: *How to get a job.*

Procedure

1. Put the students who have jobs in one or more small groups and ask them to brainstorm tips for newcomers on how to get a job. Tell them that they are the experts in this activity.
2. Have the remaining students, in small groups, brainstorm questions they would like to ask someone who has gone through the job search process.
3. After 10 minutes, regroup the students so that there is at least one expert and one questioner in each new group. If the number of experts and questioners is roughly equal, this may be done as a pair-work activity. Give the questioners 10 minutes to interview the experts and then have them write on a wall chart the most important advice that they have been given.
4. Go over the wall charts with the whole class and have the students identify the three to five most important pieces of advice.

Variation: If few or none of the students have jobs, they may move directly to the follow-up activity.

Follow-up: Have the students interview other job holders outside class. This is particularly useful if the students interview subjects who have jobs in the fields they would like to work in. The students then report back and add additional information to the wall charts, which become a resource for the whole class.

Who says what?*

Students match occupations and job-related utterances.

Time: 15 minutes
Level: High beginning and up
Main teaching points: Learn names for occupations
         Create dialogues
         Examine what different occupations involve
Organization: Pairs, whole class
Preparation: Make a sentence strip or an occupation strip for each
 member of the class (see Box 81). To accommodate different class
 sizes, more or fewer strips may be made, but it is important that in
 each case a matching strip is also distributed.

Procedure

1. Write on the blackboard, "I'm sorry I didn't do the homework." Ask
   the students the occupation of the speaker and how they know. Ask
   them for suggestions of other things that students typically say.
2. Tell them that in this activity they will be given either an occupation
   or something that someone in a particular occupation might
   typically say. If they are given an occupation, they need to find the
   student who has the corresponding sentence, and if they are given a
   sentence, they must find the person with the corresponding
   occupation.
3. When they find their partners, they should sit down together and
   create a dialogue that contains the sentence they have been given.
4. Have the students share these dialogues with the whole class.

Follow-up: Have the students make up typical sentences for their own
 jobs and share them with the class.

                     》→

---

*This activity is based on an idea in Jane Revell, *Teaching Techniques for Communicative English*, Macmillan, London, 1979.

BOX 81

Who says what? Sentence and occupation strips

Sentences	Occupations
Where do you want to go?	Taxi driver
For your safety today, we ask that you read the safety instructions in the seat pocket in front of you.	Flight attendant
Take a deep breath and hold it.	Doctor
You have two cavities	Dentist
What would you like to order?	Waitress
Open your book to page 123.	Teacher

BOX 81 (continued)

What is the prescription number?	Pharmacist
Do you know why I stopped you?	Police officer
You need a new muffler	Auto mechanic
She won't be in her office today.	Receptionist
Be sure to water it and give it lots of sun.	Plant seller
How do you want it cut?	Hairdresser
I have a person to person call for you	Telephone operator

Schedule information gap

Students ask and answer questions about work hours and duties to complete a grid.

Time: 15 minutes
Level: High beginning to intermediate
Main teaching points: Learn vocabulary related to work hours and
activities
Ask and answer questions
Organization: Pairs, groups
Preparation: Prepare enough copies of Box 82 for half the class, and enough copies of Box 83 on page 194 for the other half.

Procedure

1. Divide the class in half and distribute the form for Worker A to half the class and the form for Worker B to the other half. Subdivide the resulting groups if the class is large.
2. Ask the groups to discuss the information on their forms and to be sure they understand each item.
3. Pair students so that each pair has a form for Worker A and a form for Worker B. Tell them not to look at each other's papers.
4. Instruct the students to complete their grids by asking each other questions. They can ask as many questions as they like, but they must not look at their partners' papers.
5. When they have finished, they may check their answers by comparing their completed grids.

Variation: With lower-level students, you may want to rehearse possible questions and write them on the board before beginning the activity.
Follow-up: Students write down their own work schedules (past or present) and share them with partners.

BOX 82

Restaurant worker A

Day	Hours	Duties
Tuesday	2–10	
Wednesday		Cut lettuce and tomatoes for salad Peel potatoes Clean out the refrigerator Set tables
Thursday		
Friday		Mop kitchen Sweep dining room floor Fill water pitchers Clear tables
Saturday	12–7	Put flowers on tables Clean out the refrigerator Mop kitchen Mix bread dough
Sunday	12–6	

BOX 83

Restaurant worker B

Day	Hours	Duties
Tuesday		Clean the stove Clean the deep fat fryer Dispose of grease Put away laundry
Wednesday	2–9	
Thursday	6–10	Fill salt and pepper shakers Take out garbage Mop kitchen Mix salad dressings
Friday	4–12	
Saturday	12–7	Put flowers on tables Clean out the refrigerator Mop kitchen Mix bread dough
Sunday		Cut lettuce and tomatoes for salad Peel potatoes Mop kitchen Prepare laundry to be picked up

Interview dos and don'ts*

Students discuss rules for job interviews and formulate a list as a resource.

Time: 30 to 40 minutes
Level: Intermediate and up
Main teaching points: Learn job search skills
                       Share cultural information
                       Agree or disagree and support arguments
Organization: Individuals, groups, whole class
Preparation: Draw the dictation grid in Box 84 on the board.

Procedure

1. Ask the class to copy the dictation grid (Box 84), leaving enough room to write a sentence on each line.
2. Explain that you are going to dictate ten possible job interview rules to them. They are to write them in the long spaces on the grid. After writing each sentence, they are to indicate whether the rule should be followed *always, sometimes,* or *never* by putting a check mark in the appropriate column.
3. Read aloud the sentences in Box 85. After the students have completed the dictation, divide them into small groups. Ask them to compare and discuss their choices.
4. Have individual students write the dictated sentences on the board while the other students check for errors.
5. Then ask the groups to make up their own rules for job interviews and to report back to the whole class.
6. Draw up a list of interview rules to which everyone can agree.

Variation: If you have students who are not literate, you may pair them with students who are more advanced in writing and have them do the dictation part of the exercise together.
Follow-up: Have students ask people from the host culture the same questions and report back their answers.

                                                         ⋙→

*This activity is based on an idea in Paul Davis and Mario Rinvolucri, *Dictation*, Cambridge University Press, Cambridge, 1988.

BOX 84

Dictation grid

	Always	Sometimes	Never
1.			
2.			
3.			
4.			
5.			
6.			
7.			
8.			
9.			
10.			

BOX 85

Sentences for dictation

In an interview:

1. Ask about working hours and pay at the beginning of the interview.
2. If you don't understand a question, ask the person to repeat it.
3. Wear nice clothes.
4. Chew gum if you feel nervous.
5. Try to get some information about the employer before the interview.
6. If you don't know the answer to a question, make up something.
7. Smile and look at the interviewer.
8. Say as little as possible.
9. Ask the interviewer questions.
10. Before you go to the interview, try to guess what questions you will be asked.

Mistakes do happen

Students discuss a problem related to a pay check.

Time: 30 to 40 minutes
Level: Intermediate and up
Main teaching points: Learn how to deal with a work-related problem
        situation
        Evaluate language choices for appropriacy and
        effectiveness
        Give advice
        Use modals
Organization: Groups, whole class
Preparation: Write the problem card information (Box 86) on the board
or a large sheet of paper. Alternatively, make a copy for each student.

Procedure

1. Divide the students into small groups. Tell them to read the problem
   situation and discuss the questions.
2. Have each group write a dialogue in which Mary discusses this
   problem with her boss.
3. Have the groups read their dialogues aloud to the whole class and
   rate them for appropriateness and effectiveness.

Follow-up: Have the students brainstorm other work-related problems,
and then pick one and write a dialogue in which the problem is
addressed.

BOX 86

Problem card

Mary usually works 40 hours, but last week she worked 10 hours overtime. She wanted to use the extra money to pay for school clothes for her daughter, but when she opened her pay envelope this is what she saw:

Regular hours: 35	Overtime hours: 5
Gross pay: $1160	Insurance/Social Security: $50
Tax: $60	Net pay: $1050

What is wrong with Mary's paycheck?
Who should she talk to?
What should she say?

Calling in*

Students role-play calling in to report an absence.

Time: 30 to 40 minutes
Level: Intermediate and up
Main teaching points: Learn how to report an absence
   Respond appropriately to cues
Organization: Pairs, whole class
Preparation: Prepare enough copies of the cue cards (Box 87) for half of the students to have a card for Person A and the other half to have a card for Person B.

Procedure

1. Review language for greetings, excuses, and apologies.
2. Divide the class into pairs. Tell the students that each partner will be playing a different part in a role play based on the cards they are given. The card will not tell them the exact words to use but will tell them what they need to accomplish with the language. They may choose their own words, but they will need to respond appropriately to what their partner says.
3. Give one partner cue card A and the other cue card B. Ask the students not to allow their partners to see their cue cards. Tell them that Person A is calling Person B. Person B begins the conversation by answering the phone.
4. Give them time to go through the dialogue at least two times and then ask them to present their version to another pair.
5. Finally, ask for volunteers to present their dialogue to the whole class.
6. Discuss which language forms can be used most appropriately in this context.

Follow-up: Have the students prepare a similar dialogue dealing with apologizing for lateness.

---

*This activity is based on an idea in Jane Revell, *Teaching Techniques for Communicative English*, Macmillan, London, 1979.

BOX 87

Cue cards for calling in dialogue

Person A	Person B
B.	B. The phone rings. Answer it. Greet the caller. Identify yourself.

A. Greet B
   Identify yourself
   Apologize and say that you
   will not be at work today.
	A.

B.	B. Ask for a reason.
A. Explain your problem (give excuse).	A.

B.	B. Accept excuse.
	   Ask when B will come to
	   work.

A. Give the date or time you will return to work.	A.
B.	B. End conversation.
A. Thank A. End conversation.	A.

Point of view

Students analyze statements to determine whether they are made by a worker or a supervisor.

Time: 20 minutes
Level: Intermediate and up
Main teaching point: Consider different points of view
Organization: Pairs, whole class
Preparation: Make a set of strips (Box 88) for each pair of students. Mix the worker and supervisor strips together within each set.

Procedure

1. Divide the students into pairs and give each pair a set of strips.
2. Write the words "worker" and "supervisor" on the board. Be sure that the students understand the word "supervisor."
3. Tell the students to read each strip and to decide who is speaking. Those statements made by the worker should be put in one stack and those made by the supervisor in another.
4. With the whole class, discuss how the supervisor's point of view differs from the worker's.

BOX 88

Worker/supervisor strips

We meet every week with our supervisor.

She asks us to say what we think about our jobs.

I'm nervous about speaking English.

It's hard to understand my coworkers. By the time I understand them, they're on a new topic.

I'm afraid I'll lose my job if I say something wrong.

I want to get to know the workers better.

I want to know if people are happy or unhappy with their jobs.

I'd like to know what Maria thinks.

Maria always smiles at everybody. I'm sure she understands what they're saying.

I'd like to hear from the workers about how their workplace can be improved.

Work week

Cards are arranged as a game board and students move around the board, encountering work-related situations.

Time: 20 minutes
Level: Intermediate and up
Main teaching point: Follow directions

Work

Organization: Groups

Preparation: Make a set of game cards (Box 89) for every three or four students. Each group will also need one die. Students can supply coins to use as place markers, or the teacher can distribute colored paperclips or other small place markers.

Procedure

1. Divide the class into groups of three or four. Hand out a set of cards, a die, and place markers to each group.
2. Have each group arrange the cards in any order to form the perimeter of a square or rectangle. See Box 90.
3. Provide the directions in Box 91 orally or on the board.

BOX 89

Work week cards

You oversleep. Go back 3 spaces.	It snows and your workplace closes for 2 days. Go back 4 spaces.	You work overtime. Go ahead 2 spaces.	You fall asleep driving home from work. Go back 3 spaces.
You get a raise. Go ahead 5 spaces.	You are laid off. Go back 5 spaces.	You are sick but you forget to call your supervisor. Go back 3 spaces.	You're late because of heavy traffic. Go back 2 spaces.
You get a bonus. Move ahead 3 spaces.	You miss work because your child is sick. Go back 1 space.	Your supervisor wants you to get special training. Go ahead 4 spaces.	Your car breaks down. Go back 3 spaces.
You are named employee of the week. Go ahead 3 spaces.	WEEKEND		

Copyright © Cambridge University Press.

BOX 90

Gameboard format

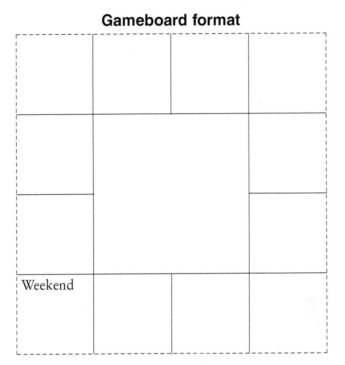

Weekend

BOX 91

Game directions

1. Decide the order in which you will take turns.
2. The "weekend" card represents the beginning and the end of the game. Put all place markers on the weekend card to begin.
3. The first player rolls his die, moves the required number of cards, reads aloud the card he lands on, and follows the directions on that card. Each player follows in turn.
4. The player to reach "weekend" first wins the game.

Mystery monologue*

Students listen to a person speak and infer who the other person is, and what the conversation is about.

Time: 15 to 20 minutes
Level: Intermediate and up
Main teaching points: Examine ways to ask for a raise
                        Infer information from fragments of text
Organization: Individuals, groups, whole class
Preparation: None

Procedure

1. Tell the students that they are going to listen to a person speaking and that their task is to work out as quickly as possible who is talking, to whom the person is speaking and why. Tell the students that you will read the monologue (Box 92) in installments and that you will ask them some questions after each installment. Encourage the students to be creative in their answers. There is no single right answer to each question.
2. Read through the monologue one installment at a time. After each installment, ask the students whether their predictions have changed, and what additional information they have gained. Other possible questions are suggested after each installment.
3. After the final installment and questions, ask the students to discuss the following questions in small groups: How is pay determined in their native countries and in their new country? Is it determined differently for different kinds of jobs? Is it usual to ask for a raise? They should also determine the best way to request a raise and then share their ideas with the whole class.

Follow-ups

1. Write and practice a dialogue asking for a raise in pay.
2. Work through mystery monologue 2 in Box 93 on page 208.
3. Have the students compose their own mystery monologues and accompanying questions.

---

*This activity is based on an idea in Colin Mortimer, *Dramatic Monologues for Listening Comprehension*, Cambridge University Press, Cambridge, 1980.

BOX 92

Mystery monologue 1

Excuse me, sir.
Who is speaking? Who is she/he talking to? What is their relationship? Where are they? What is going to happen?

Could I speak with you for a minute?
What does he/she want to talk about?
Is one speaker more important than the other?

I have been working here for almost two years now.
Where is "here"?
Who is the other person?
Does the other person know this information?

I think I have been doing a good job.
What kind of job do you think the speaker has?
Why is it important if he has been doing a good job or not?

I certainly try hard
Why is he/she saying this?

I was wondering if I could have a raise.
What will the other person say?
How does the person speaking feel?

BOX 93

Mystery monologue 2

Hello.
Who is speaking? Who is she/he talking to?

I'm sorry.
What does he/she want to talk about?
What is he/she going to say next?
What is the relationship between the speaker and the listener?

I'm going to be late today.
What is the situation?
Who is he/she speaking to?
What has happened?
Do you think that this has happened before?

My car broke down.
Why is he telling the listener this?
How will the listener respond?
How does the speaker feel?
How does the listener feel?

My brother is going to give me a ride.
Why is he/she saying this?
How does the listener feel now?

I'll be there by 9:30.
What will the other person say?
How does the person speaking feel?

Money

As students carry on their daily activities in their new country, they must learn new systems of money and banking. In addition to activities exploring the new culture, this unit also provides activities in which students compare attitudes toward money and valuables in different cultures.

Money associations

Students brainstorm words they associate with money and then decide whether the associations are positive or negative.

Time: 30 minutes
Level: Beginning and up
Main teaching points: Explore vocabulary related to money
                              Categorize
Organization: Individuals, groups, whole class
Preparation: None

Procedure

1. Brainstorm with the students words that they associate with money. Write all the words suggested on the board clarifying meanings when necessary.
2. Ask the students, working individually, to copy down the words from the board, and to put a plus sign (+) next to words that they associate positively with money ("good" words) and a minus sign (–) next to words that they associate negatively ("bad" words).
3. Have the students compare their choices in small groups.
4. Bring the whole class together and have the groups report back any disagreements and discuss further.

Money is . . .

Students explore their ideas about money.

Time: 30 minutes
Level: Beginning and up
Main teaching points: Write definitions
                        Negotiate
Organization: Individuals, pairs, groups, whole class
Preparation: None

Procedure

1. Write on the board "Money is. . . ."
2. Ask the students to think for a few minutes about how they would define money and to write down their thoughts.
3. Divide the class into pairs and have them compare their answers and try to make a definition on which they agree.
4. Put pairs together to make fours. Have each pair share the definition they wrote in step 3 and together write a definition that represents the ideas of all the group members.
5. Have each group write their final definition on the board or large pieces of paper. Discuss all the definitions with the class.

Variation: The teacher may provide a list of metaphors for money – for example, money is . . . a drug, a security blanket, a key, a mountain, power, a weapon, a lifebelt, fire, a comfortable chair. Students can then be asked to choose among them and justify their choices first in pairs and then in groups.

How much money does she have?

Students listen and write down information about money.

Time: 15 to 20 minutes
Level: High beginning to intermediate
Main teaching points: Listen and record information
Recognize and respond to cues
Organization: Groups of approximately seven students
Preparation: Make enough copies of the dictation (Box 94) and of the money strips (Box 95) so that one person in each group gets the dictation and the others get one strip each You may want to change the amounts so that they are appropriate to your location.

Procedure

1. Divide the class into groups of seven and distribute a slip of paper to each student. The groups may be smaller, with students having more than one piece of paper. The dictation slip should be given to a more advanced student.
2. Tell the student who has the dictation slip to begin reading the dictation, pausing as needed for the others to write the passage and stopping at each blank for the person who has that slip to fill in the amount.
3. At the end of the dictation, have the group members compare and check their papers.

Variation: In a lower-level class, distribute the dictation to all students and give each group member a money strip.

⫸➔

BOX 94

Dictation

Mary gets a paycheck on Friday for _____. She pays her electric bill, which is _____. Then she pays her phone bill, which is _____. She pays her rent, which is_____. She sends a money order to her parents for _____. On Saturday she goes to buy food and spends _____. How much money does she have left?

BOX 95

Money strips

Paycheck

$950

Electric bill

$45

Phone bill

$55.37

Rent

$550

Money order

$200

Food

$60.58

Checks

Students compare information about a check given in text form with the information on a filled-out check.

Time: 15 minutes
Level: High beginning to intermediate
Main teaching points: Learn how to write checks
                         Ask and answer questions
Organization: Pairs, whole class
Preparation: Make one copy of Part A (the check) for half the class and one copy of Part B (the written account) for the other half (Box 96).

Procedure

1. Draw a picture of a check on the board. Go over the parts of it with the students (date, check number, amount in numbers and words, signature).
2. Divide the class into pairs and give Part A to one of the partners and Part B to the other. Tell them not to look at their partner's paper.
3. Tell the students that the check has five errors. They are to determine what those errors are and correct them by asking each other questions. The written text is in each case the correct version.
4. When they have finished the activity, have them check their answers by looking at both papers together.

Follow-up: Have students work in pairs using the blank check provided in Box 97 on page 215 to write their own check and accompanying find-the-differences text. They can then share their materials in groups.

BOX 96

Checks worksheets

Part A: Check

0934

1/31/99

PAY TO THE
ORDER OF_____*Alan Stanton*_____ _____$25.00_____

*Twenty-five and no/hundreds*_____ DOLLARS

WORLD FIRST BANK
CAPITAL WO 63150

Part B: Written account

Check number 0944 is dated the first of January 1998. The check is written for twenty-four dollars and fifty cents. It is signed by John Stanton.

Key to errors

1. Check number. 2. The day in the date. 3. The year in the date.
4. The amount. 5. No signature.

BOX 97

Blank check

	0934
PAY TO THE	
ORDER OF_____ _____	
_____ DOLLARS	
WORLD FIRST BANK	
CAPITAL WO 63150	
	_____

Neither a borrower nor a lender be

Students discuss borrowing from and lending to particular people.

Time: 20 to 30 minutes
Level: High beginning and up
Main teaching points: Share personal opinions
Conditional constructions (*I would lend/borrow if . . .*)
Organization: Individuals, groups
Preparation: Make a copy of the borrowing grid (Box 98) for each student.

Procedure

1. List the items on the borrowing list (Box 99) on the blackboard and give each student a copy of the borrowing grid.
2. Ask the students to indicate on the grid which of the items on the list they would be prepared to borrow from or lend to each of the people on the left-hand side of the grid.
3. Have the students discuss their selections in groups, explaining the circumstances in which they would lend the items.

⟫→

BOX 98

Borrowing grid

Person	Borrow	Lend
Stranger		
Neighbor		
Acquaintance		
Best friend		
Brother		
Parents		

BOX 99

Borrowing list

1. A book
2. A pencil
3. A bicycle
4. A car
5. 25 cents
6. $5
7. $100
8. $1000
9. A credit card
10. A cup of sugar

Proverbs

Students select proverbs and explain their choices.

Time: 45 to 60 minutes
Level: High beginning and up
Main teaching points: Learn proverbs
                              Give and support opinions
Organization: Individuals and possibly groups
Preparation: Write each proverb in Box 100 on a separate piece of chart
    paper, and post them around the room

Procedure

1. Give the students time to walk around the room and read all the proverbs.
2. Ask them to stand next to the proverb that they believe is the truest and most meaningful for them.
3. They should then prepare arguments to support their choice. If other students made the same selection, they may do this as a group activity.
4. Have students or group representatives report to the whole class why they made the selections they did. Open this to whole-class discussion.

Follow-ups

1. Have groups of students think of and share additional proverbs related to money.
2. Ask students to write a paragraph explaining which proverb they chose and why.

BOX 100

Proverbs

Money doesn't grow on trees.

The best things in life are free.

A penny saved is a penny earned.

Money is the root of all evil.

Money talks.

Don't throw good money after bad.

Health is better than wealth.

Money doesn't buy happiness.

When poverty comes in the door, love flies out the window.

A fool and his money are soon parted.

Family money survey

Students ask their partners about money and families.

Time: 30 to 40 minutes
Level: High beginning and up
Main teaching points: Give personal opinions concerning family
              spending habits
              Ask and answer questions
Organization: Pairs
Preparation: Make a copy of the questionnaire (Box 101) for each
student.

Procedure

1. Divide the students into pairs and give each student a copy of the
   questions. If necessary, go over the questions to be sure everybody
   understands them.
2. Tell each student to ask his partner the questions and to record the
   responses.
3. After both partners have asked and answered the questions, have
   them compare their answers. For which ones were their answers the
   same and for which were they different?

Follow-up: Ask the questions of someone outside the class.

BOX 101

Family money survey

In your family:

Do you have a budget?
Who decides how to spend money?
Who decides about major purchases (house, car, refrigerator)?
Who does the shopping?
Who pays the bills?
Who is more careful with money, you or other members of your
family?

Where does the money go?

Students compare expenditures in their home countries and their new country using pie charts.

Time: 30 minutes
Level: High beginning and up
Main teaching points: Share cultural information
                             Make a visual representation of data
                             Use more than and less than
Organization: Individuals, pairs, whole class
Preparation: Draw the model pie chart (Box 102) on the board or on a large piece of paper, or copy it onto an overhead transparency.

Procedure

1. Show the class the model pie chart. Go over each part of it (housing, utilities, food, clothing, savings, recreation, transportation, taxes).
2. Ask the students to make two pie charts, one showing the approximate percentages spent on each item (and any other they think are necessary) in their home country and the other showing the same information for their new country.
3. Divide the students into pairs to share and discuss their pie charts. Divide them into pairs again to repeat the step.
4. Ask the whole class to discuss similarities and differences they found and to explore the reasons for them.

Variation: If students have difficulty making pie charts, they may write percentages.

BOX 102

Model pie chart

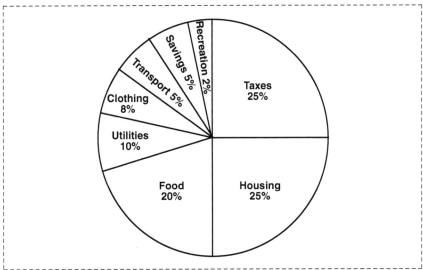

A money story

Members of a group read a story sentence by sentence and suggest what the person in the story should do.

Time: 20 to 25 minutes
Level: High beginning and up
Main teaching points: Share and support opinions
                                      Use modals
Organization: Groups of three or four students, whole class
Preparation: Prepare one set of story cards (Box 103) for each group of three or four students. Arrange them in stacks, from card 8 to card 1, so that when they are face down, card 1 will be on top.

Procedure

1. Divide the class into groups of three or four students.
2. Give each group a stack of story cards, turned upside down. The top card should be card 1.

3. Tell the students to have one person turn over the top card and read it aloud. They should discuss the top card and then repeat the process with the next one, going through the entire stack.
4. After all of the groups have finished reading and discussing the cards, go over the story with the whole class, having each group relate their thoughts on each card.

Follow-up: Write a letter to the man in the story giving him your advice and reasons for it.

Note: For a similar activity used with the theme of Family, see page 70.

BOX 103

Money story cards

1. My older brother wants to borrow some money from me.	5. My brother says he feels he can trust these men because his friend introduced them.
2. I have saved $5000 for the down payment on a house for my family.	6. These men tell him he can make a lot of money fast, but they haven't given him any details.
3. My brother says he needs $5000 to start a business.	7. They won't tell my brother their last names or their phone numbers.
4. His partners in the new business are two men he met recently in a bar.	8. He says if I give him the money, we'll both get rich. What should I do?

Lost and found

Students discuss what they would do if they found particular items.

Time: 20 minutes
Level: Intermediate and up
Main teaching points: Share and support opinions

Organization: Individuals, groups, whole class

Preparation: Cut six small pieces of paper for each class member (or have students do it themselves); write each item on the lost and found list (Box 104) on a large piece of paper to post on the wall; tape an envelope under each item.

Procedure

1. Post the lost-and-found list items and envelopes on the wall. Distribute the small pieces of paper or ask students to make them.
2. Explain to the class that they are to imagine finding each of the items on the list. They are then to decide which of the following actions they would take for each one: keep it, look for the owner, give it to the police, turn it in to the lost and found office, or other alternatives of their own choice. Using one slip of paper for each item, they should write down the action they would take and put it in the envelope below the item.
3. Divide the class into six groups. Assign each group to an item. They are to tally the responses in the envelope for their item and discuss why their classmates chose as they did.
4. Have each group report to the class.

BOX 104

Lost and found list

A diamond ring on the sidewalk

A suitcase containing $100,000 in an airport

A wallet with a name and $10 at work

A wallet with a driver's license, credit card, and $350 on the street

A wedding ring in the restroom before class

A $50 bill in the street

A $5 bill in the park

A chocolate bar on a table in the cafeteria

Write your own money survey

Students examine and answer survey questions and then write their own survey.

Time: 20 minutes
Level: Intermediate and up
Main teaching points: Share and support opinions
Ask and answer questions
Organization: Individuals, pairs, groups, whole class
Preparation: Prepare one copy of the survey (Box 105) for each student.

Procedure

1. Ask the students to answer the survey questions individually, and then have them compare their answers in groups.
2. Ask the groups to come up with additional survey questions related to money and to write these questions on the board.
3. Have each student select and write down from the board the ten questions he likes best.
4. Pair the students and have them ask each other their questions.
5. Bring the whole class back together to compare their answers.

Follow-up: Have students ask their questions to native speakers outside the class.

BOX 105

Survey questions

1. You are shopping and you see something that you really want, but you don't have the money to buy it. Do you
   a. Use a credit card to buy it now?
   b. Save money to buy it?
   c. Convince yourself that you don't need it?
   d. Other?
2. You have a date with your girlfriend or boyfriend, but you don't have any money. Would you
   a. Call her/him to cancel it?
   b. Borrow money?
   c. Tell her/him you don't have any money?
   d. Other?
3. A friend wants to borrow $100. Do you
   a. Refuse because lending money is bad for friendships?
   b. Lend him the money?
   c. Lend him the money but charge him interest?
   d. Other?
4. You see a homeless man on the street. Do you
   a. Give him some money?
   b. Ignore him?
   c. Tell him where to go to get help?
   d. Buy him some food?
   e. Other?

Bank accounts

Students acquire information about two kinds of bank accounts. (Although the information presented in this activity may not reflect local bank account systems, it is a useful example to familiarize students with some of the issues. The follow-up activity explores the local system explicitly.)

Time: 30 minutes
Level: Intermediate and up
Main teaching points: Learn about different kinds of bank accounts
                        Ask and answer questions
Organization: Pairs, whole class
Preparation: Prepare enough copies of each grid (Box 106) for half of the class. Local banks can provide similar information.

Procedure

1. Explain to the class that they will be learning about different kinds of bank accounts.
2. Divide the class into pairs. Give the form for Student A to one member of each pair and the form for Student B to the other. Neither student should look at his partner's paper.
3. Have Student A ask his partner for the information on the basic banking account and have Student B ask Student A for information on the regular checking account. When they have completed their grids, they can compare them and make corrections.
4. Discuss with the class which type of account would be best for them.

Follow-up: Students can go to local banks for information and compare it with what they learned in this activity.

BOX 106

Bank account information

Student A

	Basic Banking	**Regular Checking**
Minimum balance		$500 daily balance or $1250 average daily balance
Per check/withdrawal charge		No fee if you have the minimum balance
Monthly service fee		None
Good for:		People who can maintain the minimum balance

Student B

	Basic Banking	**Regular Checking**
Minimum balance	None	
Per check/withdrawal charge	12 free checks or withdrawals per month; 55 cents for each check or withdrawal after that	
Monthly service fee	$3	
Good for:	People who write only a few checks a month	

Pros and cons

Students compare the advantages and disadvantages of using different forms of money.

Time: 15 to 20 minutes
Level: Intermediate and up
Main teaching points: Learn about and evaluate different options for handling money
Organization: Groups, whole class
Preparation: On a large piece of paper, make the form shown in Box 107 and post it on the wall. Leave plenty of room between each form of money and in the Pros and Cons columns for writing. Make an overhead or photocopies of the forms of money and their definitions in Box 108 on page 230.

Procedure

1. Introduce the forms of money and their definitions as given in Box 108.
2. Show the students the pros and cons chart (Box 107). If the students are not familiar with the terms "pros" (good things) and "cons" (bad things), introduce them. You may want to put a small + (plus sign) next to pros and a – (minus sign) next to cons to help students remember.
3. Divide the class into small groups and assign each group one form of money. In a larger class, assign each group one form of money and either the pros or cons. Ask them to make a list of the pros and cons of using that specific kind of money.
4. When they have finished, have them fill in the large form on the wall.
5. Discuss what the groups have written, adding any further suggestions class members may have.

BOX 107

Pros and cons

Form of money	Pros	Cons
Bills		
Coins		
Personal checks		
Credit cards		
Money orders		
Traveler's checks		
Debit cards		

BOX 108

Definitions

Bills: Paper money issued by a government.

Coins: Metal money issued by a government.

Personal check: A check written on one's personal bank account.

Credit card: A card that allows one to charge purchases and pay for them at the end of the month or, with interest charges, later.

Money order: An official check, not written on a personal account. The person requesting it gives the money to the writer of the check.

Traveler's check: A check written by a large corporation in small or large denominations, which is guaranteed by the corporation in case of loss or theft.

Debit card: A card that allows one to make purchases and have the money taken directly from a bank account electronically.

Bibliography

In this brief bibliography we have chosen to focus on books that are applicable to the teaching of various languages rather than on textbooks for a specific language. We have attempted to include books that cover a range of teaching needs.

Auerbach, Elsa. (1990). *Making meaning, making change*. Boston: University of Massachusetts Press. A participatory approach to teaching adults.

Auerbach, Elsa Roberts, and Nina Wallerstein. (1987). *ESL for action*. Reading, MA: Addison-Wesley. Materials for exploring work problems in a variety of settings.

Bassano, Sharron, and Mary Ann Christison. (1995). *Community spirit: A practical guide to collaborative language learning*. Burlingame, CA: Alta Book Centers Publishers. Why and how to have a collaborative classroom.

Bell, Jill. (1988). *Teaching multilevel classes in ESL*. San Diego, CA: Dormac. Practical suggestions and activities for teaching multilevel classes.

Bell, Jill, and Barbara Burnaby. (1984). *A handbook for ESL literacy*. Toronto: Ontario Institute for Studies in Education. Theoretical and practical issues in teaching ESL to adults, particularly literacy students.

Crandall, JoAnn, and Joy Kreeft Peyton (Eds.). (1993). *Approaches to adult ESL literacy instruction*. McHenry, IL: Center for Applied Linguistics and Delta Systems. Essays on five current approaches in literacy instruction for adults.

Davis, Paul, and Mario Rinvolucri. (1988). *Dictation: New methods, new possibilities*. Cambridge, U.K.: Cambridge University Press. A variety of techniques using dictation.

Deller, Sheelagh. (1990). *Lessons from the learner*. White Plains, NY: Longman. Activities that draw on the learner's knowledge and experience.

Edge, Julian. (1989). *Mistakes and correction*. London: Longman. Practical information on how to deal with learner errors.

Gramer, Margot F. (1994). *The basic Oxford picture dictionary*. Oxford, U.K. Oxford University Press. A thematically organized dictionary with clear illustrations of useful vocabulary.

Ligon, Fred, and Elizabeth Tannenbaum. (1990). *Picture stories*. White Plains, NY: Longman. Picture stories on a variety of topics, accompanied by simple reading activities.

Lindstromberg, Seth (Ed.). (1997). *The standby book*. Cambridge, U.K.: Cambridge University Press. Activities at various levels that can be adapted for different themes.

McKay, Sandra Lee. (1993). *Agendas for second language literacy*. Cambridge, U.K.: Cambridge University Press. Analysis of the meaning and role of literacy for adults.

Moskowitz, Gertrude. (1981). *Caring and sharing in the foreign language class: A sourcebook on humanistic techniques.* Cambridge, MA: Newbury House. Activities based on students' knowledge and feelings employing a variety of modalities.

Nash, Andrea, Ann Cason, Madeline Rhum, Loren McGrail, and Rosario Gomez-Sanford. (1992). *Talking shop: A curriculum sourcebook for participatory adult ESL.* McHenry, IL: Center for Applied Linguistics and Delta Systems. A description of five teachers' experiences with participatory learning.

Nunan, David. (1992). *Designing tasks for the communicative classroom.* Cambridge, U.K.: Cambridge University Press. Useful analytical tools and guidelines for creating classroom activities.

Oxford, Rebecca. (1990). *Language learning strategies: What every teacher should know.* Boston: Heinle and Heinle. Specific activities for developing students' language learning strategies.

Palmer, Adrian, and Theodore Rodgers, with Judy Winn-Bell Olsen. (1985). *Back and forth: Pair activities for language development.* Hayward, CA: Alemany Press. Oral discrimination and information gap tasks involving pictures and text.

Raimes, Ann. (1983). *Techniques in teaching writing.* Oxford, U.K.: Oxford University Press. Useful techniques for teaching writing in a nonacademic setting.

Tom, Abigail, and Heather McKay. (1991). *The card book.* Englewood Cliffs, NJ: Prentice Hall Regents. Reproducible picture cards with accompanying activities.

Ur, Penny. (1981). *Discussions that work: Task-centered fluency practice.* Cambridge, U.K.: Cambridge University Press. Guidelines and tasks for successful discussions.

Winn-Bell Olsen, Judy. (1984). *Look again pictures for language development and lifeskills.* Hayward, CA: Alemany Press. Theme-based "find the difference" pictures with accompanying language development activities.

Wrigley, Heide Spruck, and Gloria J. A. Guth. (1992). *Bringing literacy to life.* San Diego, CA: Dominie Press. Descriptions of specific adult ESL literacy programs linking theory to practice.

Indexes

Please refer to the Contents on pages v–viii for a list of the activities in this book.

Grammar index

Function index